the barefoot contessa cookbook

the barefoot contessa cookbook

*Secrets from the
East Hampton specialty
food store for simple
food and party platters
you can make at home*

By Ina Garten

Photographs by Melanie Acevedo
Designed by Alexander Isley Inc.

CLARKSON POTTER/PUBLISHERS
NEW YORK

Copyright © 1999 by Ina Garten
Foreword copyright © 1999 by Martha Stewart
Photographs copyright © 1999 by Melanie Acevedo

Published by Clarkson Potter/Publishers,
New York, New York.
Member of the Crown Publishing Group.

Random House, Inc.
New York, Toronto, London, Sydney, Auckland
www.randomhouse.com

CLARKSON N. POTTER is a trademark and POTTER and colophon
are registered trademarks of Random House, Inc.

Printed in Japan

Library of Congress Cataloging-in-Publication Data
Garten, Ina.
The Barefoot Contessa Cookbook: secrets from the East Hampton specialty
food store for simple food and party platters you can make at home /
by Ina Garten: photographs by Melanie Acevedo.—1st ed.
Includes index.
1. Cookery.   2. Barefoot Contessa (Store)   I. Title.
TX714.G364   1999
641.5—dc21   98–7469

ISBN 0-609-60219-5

20

For my adorable husband, Jeffrey,
who always encouraged me to do
what I loved and who cheerfully
ate all those test brownies

thank you

So many people helped me create this book and I would like to thank them. First, to my dear friend, Frank Newbold, who harassed me until I agreed to start writing. I never imagined it would be so interesting. Second, to all the extraordinary people who have helped me build Barefoot Contessa: Diana Stratta, who started it all and patiently taught me how to slice smoked salmon, plus all the hundreds of wonderful people who have been with Barefoot Contessa over the last twenty years. Most important are Parker Hodges and Amy Baiata, my partners, Suzanna Guiliano, my friend and sage (as well as accountant), Harry Goodale, Paul Hodges, Shawn Miller, Alex Lazen, Peter Ranft, and Larry Hayden, who have been my other family for so long. And third, to the amazing team of people who helped me photograph this book: Melanie Acevedo, the photographer, whose eye is unequaled; Rori Spinelli, who can make a bowl of soup from a recipe for ten quarts and have it turn out absolutely perfect and beautiful; and Denise Canter, whose styling made each photograph exciting. We had a ball together and I thank them for making it all so excellent *and* fun.

Many other people were kind enough to contribute recipes: Devon Fredericks and Susan Costner, who started Loaves and Fishes in Sagaponack, New York; Eli Zabar from E.A.T., The Vinegar Factory, and Across the Street in New York City; Sarah Chase of *The Open House Cookbook;* and Brent Newsom from Brent Newsom Catering in Bridgehampton, New York. Some people let us photograph their family farms: Jim and Jennifer Pike from Pike Farms in Sagaponack, New York; Eileen and Sal Iacono from Iacono Farm in East Hampton, New York; and John, Evelyn, and Jennifer Halsey from The Milk Pail orchard in Watermill, New York. And many lent their extraordinary wares: in New York City, thanks to Herbie Schinderman from Ann Morris Antiques, Peri Wolfman from Wolfman-Gold & Good Company, Vito Giallo and Ebby Weaver at Vito Giallo Antiques, and the terrific folks at Crate & Barrel; in East Hampton, thanks to Denise Rebaudo from Curly Willow, Morley Miller from Zona, Maria Brennan from The Grand Acquisitor; and in Bridgehampton, Jane Rivkin from Kitchen Classics.

I would also like to thank Stephen Drucker, my friend and editor-in-chief of *Martha Stewart Living,* for convincing me that I really know the secrets for giving a party that is fun and for helping me put it on paper. To Cecily Stranahan, who helped me put my ideas into words. To my wonderful agent, Pam Bernstein, who believed in me from the start, and most of all, to my incomparable editor, Roy Finamore at Clarkson Potter, who guided me so brilliantly and is so much fun at lunch.

And especially, thanks to Martha Stewart, who instilled in all of us the rubric that the simplest idea is often the most delicious and beautiful; you have been a wonderful and generous friend.

Thank you all from the bottom of my heart.

contents

foreword by martha stewart 17

introduction 18

fresh ingredients for simple food 27

glossary of kitchen terms 34

appetizers 36

soups 68

salads 88

dinner 114

vegetables 144

desserts 168

breakfast 204

assembling party food 234

sources for serving platters, tableware,
and kitchen equipment 240

sources for mail-order specialty foods 246

credits 251

index 252

foreword

One meets very few people in life who combine real joie de vivre with intense curiosity, an intellectual attitude, and a serious and highly developed sense of humor. When I first encountered Ina Garten I was shopping in Barefoot Contessa, her mouth-watering specialty food store on the East End of Long Island.

Bright-eyed and apple-cheeked, Ina was immediately likable. Following her suggestions, I purchased a few of her home-baked cookies and brownies, some prepared salads, and a couple of excellent cheeses. After a few tastes I breathed a sigh of relief, now feeling assured that I would not starve, living and entertaining on the East End.

Ina and I discovered we shared many interests, most notably cooking and gardening and entertaining, as well as designing and building. Ina's husband, Jeffrey, was as friendly and interesting as Ina, and I felt a sense of comfort in their company.

When Ina and I met we were both involved with entrepreneurial ventures, and we were also both designing and building new "old" homes in East Hampton. Our conversations and discussions usually took place over relaxed breakfasts, casual lunches, or delicious dinners. It took a while, but I finally understood what motivated Ina, realizing that here was a true kindred spirit with really similar but unique talents.

I've had almost ten years to study Ina's culinary skills and philosophy about food and foodstuffs, and to taste her cooking, and I think that we are all lucky to finally have this cookbook so that we can all share these really good and tasty recipes. There is a liveliness in Ina's cooking, a total lack of finickiness, a reliance on the freshest and best, and a casualness that I know will be appealing to everyone who uses her book. Ina's love of farm-grown vegetables, backyard garden flowers and herbs, and locally produced poultry and eggs is vividly evident throughout these pages. Her intuitive cleverness in knowing what we would all like—coconut cupcakes, or maple oatmeal scones, or roasted chicken—is beautifully balanced by a very special, practical approach that makes entertaining undaunting and understandable. Ina's friendliness and her love of coddling people are so refreshing. The colorful photographs and the bright palette of the typography and book design accentuate Ina's own brilliant artistry, and her way with food is certain to become an important part of our way with food.

Martha Stewart
East Hampton
1999

intro

I had no idea what I was getting into. In 1978, I was working in the White House on nuclear energy policy and thinking there's got to be more to life than this. I came across an ad in the *New York Times* "Business Opportunities" section for a specialty food store for sale in the Hamptons, so I decided to investigate. I remembered a friend telling me, "Don't think about what you're supposed to do; think about what you enjoyed doing as a child." Cooking was what I loved to do.

So my husband, Jeffrey, and I drove up to Long Island to see this store. It was only four hundred square feet but it was love at first sight. I had no idea how to run a business or how to buy food wholesale, but I knew this was for me. I made what I thought was a low offer for the business, saying that I'd have time to rethink while we negotiated, and Jeffrey and I drove back to Washington. To my shock, the owner called the next day and said, "Thank you. I accept your offer." Yikes!

The original store had one cook and two salespeople. Twenty years later, Barefoot Contessa is a 3,000-square-foot specialty food store with twelve cooks and bakers who make salads, dinners, breads, and desserts for people to take home. Thirty people help customers choose pâtés, cheeses, smoked fish, caviar, and olive oils.

When I bought the store in the 1970s, we were all studying Julia Child's *The Art of French Cooking* like it was the Bible and we had just found religion. Each recipe had three ingredients that were recipes in

Barefoot Contessa shopping bags have become a symbol of summer in East Hampton.

Parker Hodges makes our famous sugar snap peas with sesame seeds.

themselves. Dinner for six would take days to prepare. Now I had a business to run and needed to teach people how to cook wonderful food with as little time and expense as possible.

I learned from many sources and brought my own taste to each recipe. My dear friend Anna Pump, from Loaves and Fishes in Sagaponack, Long Island, taught me that each flavor should be distinct and well balanced with other flavors. Anna also taught me that each dish needs to look like its ingredients, so our rosemary white bean soup has chunky white beans and whole rosemary in it, and the honey vanilla crème fraîche has seeds from real vanilla beans. The adorable and brilliant Eli Zabar taught me to understand what the essence of each ingredient is and to enhance it rather than mask it. His veal roast at E.A.T. in Manhattan is burnt and crusty on the outside and succulent on the inside and it's roasted with lots of fresh vegetables. Sun-dried tomatoes and goat cheese will never make that taste better! The good news is: the simpler the better. My wonderful and generous friend Martha Stewart makes everything not only taste delicious, but look beautiful without being complicated. Devon Fredericks, who owned Loaves and Fishes in the mid-1970s, was a visionary whose style of simple country food had a terrific influence on how I cook. She baked her own bread and grew her own flowers for her store before anyone heard of going back to basics.

Cooking and writing recipes is, for me, an evolutionary process. I am constantly revising the recipes I use. I believe a cookbook is just a starting place for cooks. I love to use fresh lemon juice, garlic, mustard, and caramelized onions when I cook, but you may prefer cilantro and jalapeños. I think it is very important to give recipes your own style. Use those margins by each recipe to make your own notes. Professionals don't make up recipes out of thin air; they evolve from things they've tasted or read. You can do the same thing by being a little adventurous with these recipes.

Food at Barefoot Contessa, I soon found out, is about more than dinner. It's about coming home and being taken care of. It's about Mom. I actually think that the food our mothers made may not be what we are nostalgic for. It's more an emotional picture of a mother who was always there, knew what we needed, loved us, let us run free when we wanted to explore. Food is about nurturing: not only physical but also emotional nurturing. When my best friend was working too hard, I invited him over and made him ice cream and chocolate chip cookies. Isn't that what we wanted our mothers to do? And it made me feel wonderful to be able to do it for him.

Food is not about impressing people. In fact, it's just the opposite: it's about making them feel comfortable. I invite friends to lunch and make bacon, lettuce, and tomato sandwiches. They are the best BLT's I can make, with homemade white bread, thick slabs of smokehouse bacon, tomatoes from the garden, and Hellman's mayonnaise. The meal is simpler than you expected and better than you remembered. And because

> **Recipes that are successful in the store are often the simplest.**

there are no surprises, somehow, very subtly, it makes you feel safe and comfortable. And I think that is the best setting for really connecting with people.

The recipes that are successful in the store are often the ones that are familiar but taste better than you remember. Pan-fried onion dip is like the one from Lipton's onion soup mix, but this is the real thing, with slowly cooked caramelized onions and sour cream. It's irresistible. Sure we make tomato soup, but first we roast the tomatoes to intensify their flavor, and then we stew them with lots of fresh basil leaves. Meatloaf is made the old-fashioned way, but with freshly ground turkey so it isn't so rich and heavy. And the lime tarts are baked with lime zest and freshly squeezed juice so you can taste the tartness of the fresh limes.

The most useful thing I learned by cooking professionally is that there are a million things that you can do in advance to make cooking less stressful. Cheddar dill scones can be mixed, cut into squares, and refrigerated for a week before they are baked for breakfast. Grilled salmon salad ingredients can be prepared separately from the dressing and then mixed with vegetables and seasoned at the last minute. Our French potato salad tastes *better* if it is left in the refrigerator for a day so the vinaigrette soaks into the potatoes. I have learned how to prepare everything in advance so I'm not a wreck when my guests arrive. There are notes throughout the book to help you save time and avoid stress.

A word about party platters. We all want gorgeous food that we can just put on a buffet table and let our guests help themselves, but they look too complicated to make ourselves. The secret is that they're very easy to make! And there's no reason you have to make everything you put on the platter. Every town has

Make it easy on yourself.

opposite: The invitation at the entrance to the Milk Pail orchard is hard to pass up.

special treats you can discover and take out. There's a cheese store where you can buy wonderful cheeses for making a fruit and cheese platter; a specialty food store for grilled vegetables to make a vegetable platter; and a bakery for cookies and lemon bars to make a country dessert platter. Or you can bake your own shortbread hearts and fill in with brownies and long-stemmed strawberries you've bought. With photographs to inspire you and instructions to help you design platters, you'll soon feel just like a professional.

At Barefoot Contessa we've made hundreds of thousands of banana crunch muffins over the years, so I *know* the recipe works. Grilled salmon salad, sugar snap peas with black sesame seeds, and fresh corn salad with basil—these are the dishes that have made the store so popular over the years, and you can make them at home exactly as we make them at the store. Party dishes like roasted salmon with fennel, spinach pie, and pecan shortbread can wow your own guests. When I find recipes that work, I use them over and over again. I hope the recipes in these pages will please you so much that they enter your repertoire, too. Enjoy!

opposite: Harry Goodale pats out the dough for pecan bars.

Jim Pike's fresh berries are delicious with our honey vanilla crème fraîche.

fresh
ingredients for
simple
food

A year ago, I spent two weeks at a fabulous house in Provence. I went with grand notions of spending my time making bouillabaisse on the La Cornue stove, pissaladière in the wood-burning oven, slow-cooked stocks, and elaborate desserts. But that's not how it worked out. It was August and everything at the market was so beautiful and fresh. Little fingerling potatoes, bright red radishes, and tiny sweet carrots still had soil clinging to them. Tomatoes and zucchini had been picked in the morning after ripening on the vine. Fraise des bois and raspberries were intense and sweet. We got fresh baguettes,

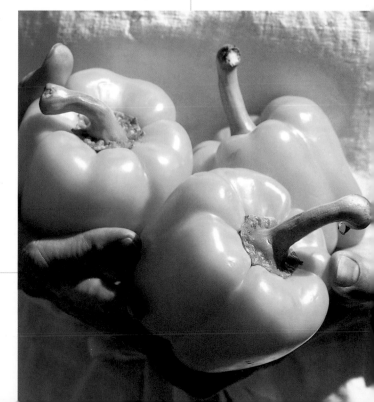

big ripe tomatoes, a slice of runny Vacherin cheese, tiny home-made saucissons, and juicy white peaches. Who needed to cook? The most we ever did was boil fresh potatoes and drizzle them with fruity olive oil and lots of coarse salt and pepper. Fire up the oven? I don't think so.

I try as much as possible to base my cooking on ingredients that come from local sources: chickens from the Iaconos' farm in East Hampton, apples from The Milk Pail orchard in Watermill, fresh local fish from the Wainscott Seafood Shop, and homegrown vegetables from Jim Pike's farm in Sagaponack. I am very lucky to live in a rural area where these resources are available, but everyone has some access to fresh food. Look around and see what is made locally and base your menus on those ingredients: a smokehouse that makes wonderful bacon and ham, an Italian store that makes its own special sausages, an orchard for pears and apples, or a farmer's market for fresh milk and cheeses. Even if you can't find any of these

Apples always taste better when you pick them yourself.

Ripe tomatoes need only a splash of balsamic vinegar and coarse salt to serve for dinner.

nearby, you can turn to the incredible array of ingredients available by mail from producers all over the country: I have listed many of my favorite sources in the appendix, but keep your eyes open for others when you read newspapers and magazines.

The menu at Barefoot Contessa has always been built on simple, fresh, seasonal food. The key to delicious simple food is, of course, to use the best ingredients. It can't be said enough. Don't just buy the reddest strawberries; ask to taste one. You'll be surprised how much that focuses your attention on the quality of the ingredients. There are, of course, things you can't taste, like potatoes and melons. Smell them, feel them, but most important of all, buy them in season and buy them from the source. Little fingerling potatoes are freshest in the late summer and autumn; tomatoes and basil are great between July and October, but I think they are the sweetest in September. Experiment with different ingredients: I often buy one each of five different potatoes, which I boil to see

Hands are a cook's best utensils.

opposite: Haas avocados are the ugly brown ones, but they make the best guacamole.

which one has the best texture and flavor: then I will base meals for the rest of the winter on that variety.

The same holds true for kitchen staples. I am always testing olive oils and finding the ones with the freshest fruity olive flavors. I am obsessive about mayonnaise—for me, Hellman's or Best's clearly has the most flavor. Salts and peppers vary: I use kosher salt or sea salt and I grind Tellicherry black peppercorns. Even curry powder can be boring and flat, or it can have a wonderful depth of flavor and subtle spice. There are notes throughout the book with the brands we like at Barefoot Contessa, and there are margins next to each recipe so you can write in your own favorites.

fresh lemonade

MAKES 1½ QUARTS

Lemonade is the quintessential flavor of summer and epitomizes the notion of fresh ingredients for simple food. There are so many bad imitations around and the real thing is so easy to make. We like to add a few slices of lemon to each pitcher, or you can just toss in a few squeezed lemon halves.

1 CUP *freshly squeezed lemon juice (5 to 6 lemons)*
½–¾ CUP *superfine sugar, to taste*
1 CUP *crushed ice*
4 CUPS *water*

Place all the ingredients in a blender and process until completely smooth. Serve over ice.

glossary of kitchen terms

Kitchen terms like *chop* and *dice* sometimes seem vague. These photographs show how we at Barefoot Contessa would follow those directions.

A   Julienne

B   Mince

C   Small-Dice

D   Medium-Dice

E   Chop

F   Chiffonade

appetizers

Roasted Eggplant Spread

Lamb Sausage in Puff Pastry

Lobster Salad in Endive

Crab Cakes
  with Rémoulade Sauce

Hummus

Grilled Lemon Chicken
  with Satay Dip

Guacamole

Pan-Fried Onion Dip

Sun-Dried Tomato Dip

Smoked Salmon Tea Sandwiches

Turkey Tea Sandwiches

Vegetable Sushi

Fruit and Cheese Platter

the cocktail party

Before I owned a specialty food store, I could spend hours making hors d'oeuvres for a cocktail party. Now I think it's more important to have fun and to spend time with my friends. If I am racing around getting drinks for everyone and then running back and forth to the kitchen to get hot hors d'oeuvres out of the oven, I have missed the point of having a party. So now I have several guidelines for myself.

First, all the fixings for drinks are on a table in the room where cocktails are served: glasses, wines, alcohol, mixers, ice, lemons, and limes. I often have one special drink which everyone ends up choosing: Campari with soda and blood orange juice, champagne and crème de cassis, or margaritas. Second, I do everything possible to ensure that I never leave the room. Friends need to be greeted, people who don't know each other need to be introduced, and the energy of a party is set from the moment people arrive. I choose appetizers that can be served at room temperature and everything is out on tables or ready to pass before the first guest arrives. Third, despite my passion for good food, it's not my first priority for a good cocktail party. The first one is the guest list. Are the people interesting? Will they enjoy each other's company? Are there surprises? I sometimes ask people to bring friends who are fun so surprises happen.

Cocktail parties with good, hearty food can be a very easy way to entertain, particularly on Friday night. I serve five or six different kinds of appetizers and three of each kind per person. Plan a menu like a meal: seafood (crab cakes), vegetables (roasted eggplant), and meat (chicken satay). You can even serve coffee and a country dessert platter at the end. Friends stop on their way home from work—who needs dinner after a good cocktail party?—and they can be home by 9:30, having had a wonderful start to their weekend.

roasted eggplant spread

SERVES 6 TO 8

This is not only good, it's good for you. Many years ago we developed a group of recipes that have almost no fat for customers who like to save their calories for dessert. I love to serve this alongside other Mediterranean specialties, such as hummus, pita bread, Greek olives, feta cheese, and stuffed grape leaves.

1   *medium eggplant, peeled*

2   *red bell peppers, seeded*

1   *red onion, peeled*

2   *garlic cloves, minced*

3 TABLESPOONS   *good olive oil*

1½ TEASPOONS   *kosher salt*

½ TEASPOON   *freshly ground black pepper*

1 TABLESPOON   *tomato paste*

Preheat the oven to 400 degrees.

Cut the eggplant, bell pepper, and onion into 1-inch cubes. Toss them in a large bowl with the garlic, olive oil, salt, and pepper. Spread them on a baking sheet. Roast for 45 minutes, until the vegetables are lightly browned and soft, tossing once during cooking. Cool slightly.

Place the vegetables in a food processor fitted with a steel blade, add the tomato paste, and pulse 3 or 4 times to blend. Taste for salt and pepper.

The cloves of elephant garlic, which you find in specialty stores, are easier to peel, but I prefer the more intense flavor of the common type of garlic.

lamb sausage in puff pastry

MAKES 28 APPETIZERS; SERVES 6 TO 8

Whenever I am catering a party and the husband wants good old "pigs in blankets" and the wife wants something more sophisticated, I recommend lamb sausage in puff pastry. It looks the same but tastes so much better. You can use any kind of thin fresh sausage for this recipe. I like to serve it with extra mustard.

1 POUND	*fresh lamb sausage, ¹/₂ inch thick, in a coil*
2 SHEETS	*commercial puff pastry, thawed (see note)*
2 TABLESPOONS	*Dijon mustard*
1	*egg, beaten with 1 tablespoon water or milk, for egg wash*

Find a store that makes their own sausage and try different kinds.

One package of Pepperidge Farm puff pastry (17¼ ounces) has two sheets.

This appetizer can be assembled a day ahead, refrigerated, and baked just before serving.

Preheat the oven to 400 degrees.

Bake the sausage on a baking sheet for 20 minutes. Turn the sausage and bake it 5 to 10 minutes more, until it's fully cooked. Cool to room temperature.

Unfold the puff pastry on a lightly floured board. Cut each piece in half lengthwise and brush the top sides with mustard. Divide the sausage into 4 equal pieces. Starting at the long end of the pastry, place 1 piece of the sausage on top of the mustard and roll it up tightly, overlapping the end by ¹/₂ inch and sealing the pastry by brushing the edge with water. Cut off the excess pastry. Roll the other 3 pieces of sausage in puff pastry. Place the 4 rolls, seam side down, on a baking sheet lined with parchment paper. Brush with the egg wash. Lightly score each roll diagonally to make 7 equal pieces. Bake at 400 degrees for 20 to 25 minutes, until browned. Slice and serve immediately.

lobster salad in endive

MAKES 24 APPETIZERS; SERVES 6 TO 8

If you want to be good to yourself and your guests at the same time, ask your fish store to sell you cooked fresh lobster meat, instead of cooking a lobster yourself. This is a great summer appetizer or a special treat for New Year's Eve. This recipe is also good, and not quite so expensive, with cooked shrimp or crabmeat. You'll see that a little salad makes a lot of appetizers.

¾ POUND	*fresh cooked lobster meat, small-diced*
½ CUP	*good mayonnaise*
½ CUP	*small-diced celery (1 stalk)*
1 TABLESPOON	*capers, drained*
1½ TABLESPOONS	*minced fresh dill*
PINCH	*kosher salt*
PINCH	*freshly ground black pepper*
4 HEADS	*Belgian endive*

Combine the lobster, mayonnaise, celery, capers, dill, salt, and pepper.

With a sharp knife, cut off the base of the endive and separate the leaves. Use a teaspoon to fill the end of each endive leaf with lobster salad. Arrange on a platter and serve.

To cook lobsters, drop them in a large pot of boiling water, cover, bring the water back to a boil, and wait 10 minutes. Take the lobsters out and allow them to cool before removing the meat from the shell. Three 1¼-pound lobsters will make about ¾ pound of lobster meat.

crab cakes

MAKES ABOUT 26 MINI CRAB CAKES; SERVES 6 TO 8

Crab cakes are always good for dinner or in sandwiches for lunch, but I like them best as finger food. You can make them ahead, chill them, and then fry them before serving. When we cater a party, this is always the first appetizer to go. They are wonderful with Rémoulade Sauce.

2 TABLESPOONS	unsalted butter
2 TABLESPOONS	olive oil
¾ CUP	small-diced red onion (1 small onion)
1½ CUPS	small-diced celery (4 stalks)
½ CUP	small-diced red bell pepper (1 small pepper)
½ CUP	small-diced yellow bell pepper (1 small pepper)
¼ CUP	minced fresh flat-leaf parsley
1 TABLESPOON	capers, drained
¼ TEASPOON	Tabasco sauce
½ TEASPOON	Worcestershire sauce
1½ TEASPOONS	Old Bay Seasoning
½ TEASPOON	kosher salt
½ TEASPOON	freshly ground black pepper
½ POUND	lump crabmeat, drained and picked to remove shells
½ CUP	plain dry bread crumbs
½ CUP	good mayonnaise
2 TEASPOONS	Dijon mustard
2	extra-large eggs, lightly beaten

FOR FRYING

4 TABLESPOONS	unsalted butter
¼ CUP	olive oil

Place the 2 tablespoons butter, 2 tablespoons oil, onion, celery, red and yellow bell peppers, parsley, capers, Tabasco sauce, Worcestershire sauce, Old Bay Seasoning, salt, and pepper in a large sauté pan over medium-low heat and cook until the vegetables are soft, approximately 15 to 20 minutes. Cool to room temperature. In a large bowl, break the lump crabmeat into small pieces and toss with the bread crumbs, mayonnaise, mustard, and eggs. Add the cooked mixture and mix well. Cover and chill in the refrigerator for 30 minutes. Shape into bite-sized crab cakes.

Heat the butter and olive oil for frying over medium heat in a large sauté pan. Add the crab cakes and fry for 4 to 5 minutes on each side, until browned. Drain on paper towels; keep them warm in a 250-degree oven and serve hot.

Crab cakes can be shaped and stored overnight in the fridge on baking sheets wrapped in plastic. Fry just before serving.

rémoulade sauce

MAKES ³/₄ CUP

This sauce is more traditional with celeriac as a salad, but I love to use it with crab cakes. It is like tartar sauce, but with much more flavor. Serve cold or at room temperature.

This is also delicious as a dip for cold shrimp or as a sauce for grilled fish.

½ CUP	*good mayonnaise*
2 TABLESPOONS	*small-diced pickles or cornichons*
1 TEASPOON	*coarse-grained mustard*
1 TABLESPOON	*champagne or white wine vinegar*
PINCH	*kosher salt*
PINCH	*freshly ground black pepper*

Place all the ingredients in a food processor fitted with a steel blade and pulse several times until the pickles are finely chopped and all the ingredients are well mixed but not puréed.

hummus

MAKES 2 CUPS

At Barefoot Contessa we make a very lemony hummus with lots of garlic and spice. I like to drizzle it with olive oil, sprinkle it with toasted pignoli, and serve it as a dip for pita bread and endive leaves. This is very quick to make and lasts for a week in the refrigerator.

2 CUPS	*canned chickpeas, drained, liquid reserved*
1½ TEASPOONS	*kosher salt*
4	*garlic cloves, minced*
⅓ CUP	*tahini (sesame paste)*
6 TABLESPOONS	*freshly squeezed lemon juice (2 lemons)*
2 TABLESPOONS	*water or liquid from the chickpeas*
8 DASHES	*Tabasco sauce*

Place all the ingredients in the bowl of a food processor fitted with a steel blade and process until the hummus is coarsely puréed. Taste for seasoning and serve chilled or at room temperature.

Tahini is available at supermarkets and specialty food stores.

There is no substitute for freshly squeezed lemon juice. Any other product tastes artificial and ruins the flavor of hummus.

Lemons at room temperature produce more juice than cold ones.

grilled lemon chicken

SERVES 8 TO 10

This is a famous Barefoot Contessa recipe. I'd hate to have to add up how many millions of pounds of grilled lemon chicken we have made over the years. We use this as an appetizer, as shown here with a peanuty satay dip, but we also mix it with vegetables and a fresh lemon vinaigrette for lunch or serve whole grilled chicken breasts for a delicious and healthy dinner. The longer you marinate the chicken, the better. Serve warm with Satay Dip (recipe follows).

Crushing dried herbs with your hands releases the flavor.

¾ CUP	*freshly squeezed lemon juice (4 lemons)*
¾ CUP	*good olive oil*
2 TEASPOONS	*kosher salt*
1 TEASPOON	*freshly ground black pepper*
1 TABLESPOON	*minced fresh thyme leaves (½ teaspoon dried)*
2 POUNDS	*boneless chicken breasts, halved and skin removed*

Whisk together the lemon juice, olive oil, salt, pepper, and thyme. Pour over the chicken breasts in a nonreactive bowl. Cover and marinate in the refrigerator for 6 hours or overnight.

Heat a charcoal grill and cook the chicken breasts for 10 minutes on each side, until *just* cooked through. Cool slightly and cut diagonally in ½-inch-thick slices.

Skewer with wooden sticks.

satay dip

MAKES 1½ CUPS

Inspiration for this recipe came from a wonderful caterer in Philadelphia who wrote The Frog Commissary Cookbook. *I love the complexity of the flavor in this recipe, which is so quick to make.*

1 TABLESPOON	*good olive oil*
1 TABLESPOON	*dark sesame oil*
⅔ CUP	*small-diced red onion (1 small onion)*
1½ TEASPOONS	*minced garlic (2 cloves)*
1½ TEASPOONS	*minced fresh ginger root*
¼ TEASPOON	*crushed red pepper flakes*
2 TABLESPOONS	*good red wine vinegar*
¼ CUP	*light brown sugar, packed*
2 TABLESPOONS	*soy sauce*
½ CUP	*smooth peanut butter*
¼ CUP	*ketchup*
2 TABLESPOONS	*dry sherry*
1½ TEASPOONS	*freshly squeezed lime juice*

Cook the olive oil, sesame oil, red onion, garlic, ginger root, and red pepper flakes in a small, heavy-bottomed pot on medium heat until the onion is transparent, 10 to 15 minutes. Whisk in the vinegar, sugar, soy sauce, peanut butter, ketchup, sherry, and lime juice; cook for 1 more minute. Cool and use as a dip for Grilled Lemon Chicken skewers.

We use Kikkoman soy sauce.

Freshly squeezed lime juice makes all the difference.

You can find dark sesame oil in Asian stores. It tastes just like roasted sesame seeds rather than a plain, flavorless oil.

This dip will last for a month in the refrigerator.

guacamole

MAKES 3 CUPS

We use a knife to chop the avocados, which makes a chunky dip. It is very important to use Haas avocados from California. They're not the pretty green ones you see in the market, but the earthy brown ones. They are ripe when they just give to the touch. I am not a cilantro fan, so add it if you love it. Serve at room temperature with yellow or blue corn chips.

4	*ripe Haas avocados*
3 TABLESPOONS	*freshly squeezed lemon juice (1 lemon)*
8 DASHES	*Tabasco sauce*
½ CUP	*small-diced red onion (1 small onion)*
1	*large garlic clove, minced*
1 TEASPOON	*kosher salt*
1 TEASPOON	*freshly ground black pepper*
1	*medium tomato, seeded, and small-diced*

Cut the avocados in half, remove the pits, and scoop the flesh out of their shells into a large bowl. (I use my hands.) Immediately add the lemon juice, Tabasco, onion, garlic, salt, and pepper and toss well. Using a sharp knife, slice through the avocados in the bowl until they are finely diced. Add the tomatoes. Mix well and taste for salt and pepper.

A customer once asked us, "How do you get the guacamole green?" Of course we wondered what color it should be, but I think she wanted to know how we got it so green. We keep it green by storing it with plastic wrap pressed directly on top. Air will turn it brown, so the less air contact, the better. I believe it's only a myth that an avocado pit will keep the guacamole green. Lemon juice does the best job.

Caramelized onions and sour cream for onion dip plus home-made potato chips.

pan-fried onion dip

MAKES 2 CUPS

This dip is like the California dip we remember from our childhood, except it's the real thing, with slowly caramelized onions, and it's ten times more tasty. For a real treat, I love to serve this appetizer with Eli Zabar's potato chips plus fresh vegetables and crackers for dipping.

2	*large yellow onions*
4 TABLESPOONS	*unsalted butter*
¼ CUP	*vegetable oil*
¼ TEASPOON	*ground cayenne pepper*
1 TEASPOON	*kosher salt*
½ TEASPOON	*freshly ground black pepper*
4 OUNCES	*cream cheese, room temperature*
½ CUP	*sour cream*
½ CUP	*good mayonnaise*

Cut the onions in half, and then slice them into ⅛-inch-thick half-rounds. (You will have about 3 cups of onions.)

Heat the butter and oil in a large sauté pan on medium heat. Add the onions, cayenne, salt, and pepper and sauté for 10 minutes. Reduce the heat to medium-low and cook, stirring occasionally, for 20 more minutes, until the onions are browned and caramelized. Allow the onions to cool.

Place the cream cheese, sour cream, and mayonnaise in the bowl of an electric mixer fitted with a paddle attachment and beat until smooth. Add the onions and mix well. Taste for seasonings.

Serve at room temperature.

By combining butter and oil, you get the best properties of each: the flavor of butter and the high smoking point of oil.

sun-dried tomato dip

MAKES 2 CUPS

Here is the most popular dip we make at Barefoot Contessa. Reminiscent of Russian dressing, it is updated with the intense flavors of sun-dried tomatoes and fresh scallions. This takes virtually a minute to make and can be served with crackers, chips, and fresh vegetables.

¼ CUP	*sun-dried tomatoes in oil, drained and chopped (8 tomatoes)*
8 OUNCES	*cream cheese, room temperature*
½ CUP	*sour cream*
½ CUP	*good mayonnaise*
10 DASHES	*Tabasco sauce*
1 TEASPOON	*kosher salt*
¾ TEASPOON	*freshly ground black pepper*
2	*scallions, thinly sliced (white and green parts)*

Room-temperature cream cheese ensures that the dip won't have lumps.

The white part of the scallion has the most flavor, but the green also has flavor and it adds color and texture to the dip.

Purée the tomatoes, cream cheese, sour cream, mayonnaise, Tabasco sauce, salt, and pepper in a food processor fitted with a metal blade. Add the scallions and pulse twice. Serve at room temperature.

smoked salmon tea sandwiches

MAKES 32 SANDWICHES; SERVES 8 TO 10

Tea sandwiches are wonderful for a cocktail party or an afternoon tea. They can be made a day ahead and kept refrigerated, covered with damp paper towels and wrapped in plastic to keep them moist. We often make platters with several types of tea sandwiches, but these are always the first to go.

HERB BUTTER

½ POUND	unsalted butter, room temperature
¼ TEASPOON	minced garlic
1 TABLESPOON	minced scallions (white and green parts)
1 TABLESPOON	minced fresh dill
1 TABLESPOON	minced fresh flat-leaf parsley
1 TEASPOON	freshly squeezed lemon juice
1 TEASPOON	kosher salt
¼ TEASPOON	freshly ground black pepper

SANDWICHES

1 LOAF	dense 7-grain or health bread, unsliced
8 SLICES	smoked salmon

If you use only a single layer of salmon, the sandwiches will hold together well.

For the herb butter, combine all the butter ingredients in a mixer fitted with a paddle attachment. Beat until mixed, but do not whip.

For the sandwiches, have the store slice the bread lengthwise on a meat slicer into ¼-inch-thick slices. (If that isn't possible, you can slice it crosswise with a very sharp knife.)

Lay out 8 slices of bread and spread them all with a thin layer of herb butter. Place smoked salmon on 4 of the slices. Top with the other 4 slices of bread, butter side down. Place the sandwiches on a baking sheet and wrap with plastic. Refrigerate until the butter is very cold. Place the sandwiches on a cutting board. With a very sharp knife, cut off the crusts, cut each large sandwich in half crosswise, and then cut each half diagonally twice to make a total of 8 small triangles. (If the bread was cut crosswise, follow the assembly directions, then cut off the crusts and cut diagonally, twice, to make 4 small triangles.) Serve chilled.

I use Health Bread from Eli's Bread for my tea sandwiches.

turkey tea sandwiches

MAKES 32 SANDWICHES; SERVES 8 TO 10

What an unusual combination for a sandwich! I invented it for a picnic lunch, and people loved it so much I decided to put it on the menu. Fresh basil leaves are the secret. These sandwiches can be made a day ahead and refrigerated, covered with damp paper towels and wrapped in plastic to keep them moist.

SCALLION CREAM CHEESE

¾ POUND	cream cheese, room temperature
½ CUP	minced scallions (white and green parts)

SANDWICHES

1 LOAF	dense raisin-nut bread, unsliced
8	thin slices fresh or smoked turkey breast
	Fresh basil leaves

I use Eli's Raisin Pecan Bread.

Water turns basil leaves brown. To store basil, wash the leaves well, and then spin them very dry in a salad spinner. Put the leaves in a plastic storage bag with a paper towel to absorb any extra moisture. The leaves will stay fresh and green for several days.

For the scallion cream cheese, combine the cream cheese and scallions in an electric mixer fitted with a paddle attachment. Do not whip.

For the sandwiches, have the store slice the bread lengthwise on a meat slicer into ¼-inch-thick slices. (If that isn't possible, you can slice it crosswise with a very sharp knife.)

Lay out 8 slices of bread and spread them all with a thin layer of scallion cream cheese. Place a single layer of turkey on half the slices, cutting the edges to fit the bread. Place the basil leaves randomly on top of the turkey. Top with the other 4 slices of bread, cream cheese side down. Lay the sandwiches on a baking sheet, and wrap the sheet with plastic. Refrigerate until the cream cheese is cold and firm. Place the sandwiches on a cutting board and, with a very sharp knife, cut off the crusts. Cut each large sandwich in half crosswise, and then cut each half diagonally, twice, to make a total of 8 small triangles. (If the bread was cut crosswise, follow the assembly directions, then cut off the crusts and cut diagonally, twice, to make 4 small triangles.) Serve chilled.

You can also just cut the sandwiches into fingers.

vegetable sushi

MAKES 40 APPETIZERS; SERVES 10 TO 12

This is a very popular hors d'oeuvre at Barefoot Contessa. It takes a few tries to get the hang of the rolling, but it's worth the effort. Try different fillings like crabmeat or smoked salmon and you can have lots of varieties from one recipe.

1¼ POUNDS	*sushi rice (2³⁄4 cups)*
3 CUPS	*water*
¼ CUP	*mirin, plus additional for moistening nori*
5 SHEETS	*nori (1 package)*
4 TEASPOONS	*wasabi powder, mixed with 2 teaspoons water*
½ CUP	*small-diced red onion*
1	*carrot, julienned*
1	*red bell pepper, julienned*
1	*yellow bell pepper, julienned*
1	*scallion, julienned (green part only)*
1	*hothouse cucumber, seeded and julienned*
1	*10-ounce jar pickled ginger*
	Sushi Dipping Sauce (recipe follows)

Place the rice in a strainer and rinse under cold running water until the water is fairly clear, about 5 minutes. Shake the water out and allow the rice to dry in the strainer for 15 minutes.

Put the rice in a pot with exactly 3 cups of water and cook covered on high heat until it starts to foam, about 5 minutes. Reduce the heat to low and cook until tender, about 15 minutes. Turn off the heat and sprinkle with 1/4 cup mirin. Replace the

continued next page

lid and allow the rice to steam for 15 minutes. Place in a bowl and cool to room temperature.

To prepare the sushi, place a bamboo sushi roller flat on a table with the bamboo reeds horizontal to you. Sprinkle lightly with water. Place one nori sheet on top, smooth side down, and moisten lightly with mirin. With damp hands, press 1¼ cups rice flat on top of the nori, leaving 1½-inch edges on the top and bottom, but pressing all the way to the sides. Make sure the rice is pressed even and smooth.

Spread ¼ teaspoon of wasabi paste in a horizontal stripe near the lower edge of the rice. Over the wasabi, lightly sprinkle the onions in a horizontal stripe. Place strips of carrots in a horizontal stripe, on top of the wasabi and onions, and follow by piling the red and yellow peppers, scallions, and cucumbers on top, making a tight, straight bundle of vegetables. Place one layer of pickled ginger slices on top.

Don't worry about using all of the fillings; you'll have some left over to make more rolls later.

To roll the sushi, pick up the near edge of the bamboo roller and hold it with the nori, then pull them up and over the vegetable bundle until the nori reaches the rice on the other side. Press the roller to make a round bundle, then roll the bundle to the far edge of the nori and press again to make a round bundle. (The nori should totally enclose the rice and vegetables in a round tube, but the ends will have rice and vegetables sticking out.) Repeat the process with the remaining ingredients.

Keep the rolls under a damp towel and refrigerate until ready to serve. To serve, slice off the ends with a very sharp knife and slice each roll into 8 equal pieces. Place on a platter and serve with more pickled ginger and Sushi Dipping Sauce.

sushi dipping sauce

½ TEASPOON	*wasabi powder*
¼ TEASPOON	*water*
½ TEASPOON	*crushed red pepper flakes*
1 TEASPOON	*minced pickled ginger*
1 TEASPOON	*minced scallion (green part only)*
¼ CUP	*white wine vinegar*
3 TABLESPOONS	*good soy sauce*
½ TEASPOON	*dark sesame oil*

Combine the wasabi powder and water to make a paste. Mix in the red pepper flakes, ginger, scallions, vinegar, soy sauce, and sesame oil. Serve as a dip with the sushi.

fruit and cheese platter

Assembling a stunning fruit and cheese platter requires no cooking. I follow a few key principles to be sure it looks festive and is easy for guests to help themselves. First, I choose an interesting assortment of cheeses—hard sharp cheeses, soft creamy ones, and pungent blue cheeses. I look for an interesting mix of flavors, textures, and colors. For example, in this photograph I used ripe French Camembert; Le Chevrot, a sharp goat cheese; Rondin with herbs, a creamy goat cheese; and Montagnolo, a creamy blue cheese.

Go to the best cheese shop in town and ask the person at the counter which cheeses are ready to serve. Taste everything; they expect you to. We all know that the Brie may look terrific, but it can be underripe and tough or overripe and ammoniated. You want only the freshest cheeses that are perfectly ripened. Take them home, refrigerate them, and then bring them to room temperature a few hours before serving.

Second, be sure to have a platter or wooden board that is flat and large enough to hold the cheeses without crowding them. Arrange the cheeses with the cut sides facing out, and with several small cheese knives, maybe one for each type of cheese.

Third, choose very simple fruit. A large bunch of green or red grapes placed slightly off center anchors the design and gives it height. Then you can add other seasonal fruit—fresh apricots, Seckel pears, strawberries, or figs. I sometimes like to add dried dates, dried apricots, or roasted cashews.

Last, to finish the platter, add sliced breads or crackers, and green leaves. I use either lemon or galax leaves, which you can get from your florist. If you have a garden, any large flat leaf like hydrangea looks beautiful, but be sure they aren't poisonous and are pesticide-free!

Always look for the freshest, crustiest breads.

Overall, the simpler the design, the better the platter looks. Group each kind of fruit together and create a visual focal point. Red grapes or strawberries draw your eye to the center. Fill in the spaces with lots of crackers or small slices of bread.

soups

Parker's Split Pea Soup

Cheddar Corn Chowder

French Onion Soup

Roasted-Potato Fennel Soup

Gazpacho

Lentil Vegetable Soup

Rosemary White Bean Soup

Roasted-Tomato Basil Soup

Parmesan Croutons

soup for lunch

The most healing food I know is soup. When I'm down, I love to get some fresh chickens from Mr. Iacono's farm and lots of fresh vegetables from the farmstand and make a huge pot of chicken stock. Just the smell makes me feel better, and a big bowl of chicken soup with vegetables and shredded chicken is sure to raise my spirits. Now, why wouldn't that be good for my friends, too?

So let's talk about Sunday lunch, my favorite meal for entertaining. Everyone is done with their Saturday chores and Sunday night is still ahead, so thoughts of work are far away. People have more energy. But, best of all, Sunday lunch can be soup—cold, chunky gazpacho with Parmesan croutons in summer, hot cheddar corn chowder in September when the corn is sweetest, and roasted-potato fennel soup on the coldest snowy day. All you need to make is a big salad, with fruit and cheese for dessert, and everyone goes home feeling "all better" to deal with the dragons of the coming week.

Soup is also easy for the cook. Most of my soups start with sautéed onions to give a sweet, rich flavor to the stock, and then you can add anything you want, including your leftovers from last night's dinner. A friend of mine says it's the only way to get vegetables into her children; every week she empties the contents of the refrigerator's vegetable bin into a large pot with chicken stock and makes a puréed vegetable soup so delicious and satisfying that the kids never know that it's good for them.

Recipes that call for chicken stock will taste better with homemade stock, but if you are in a hurry, use a good canned stock. In this chapter I've included many of the most popular soup recipes at Barefoot Contessa. I hope they'll be popular in your house, too.

parker's split pea soup

SERVES 10 TO 12

Parker Hodges is the extraordinary chef at Barefoot Contessa. When he makes this split pea soup, he cooks most of the split peas in the stock, but then he adds more halfway through the cooking to give this hearty soup terrific flavor and texture. Chicken stock gives the soup a richer flavor than water, but either way this soup is incredibly satisfying. Serve this with a garnish of croutons or diced smoked ham. Steven Spielberg told me this tastes just like his mother's.

2 CUPS	*chopped yellow onions (2 onions)*
1 TABLESPOON	*minced garlic (3 cloves)*
¼ CUP	*good olive oil*
1 TEASPOON	*dried oregano*
1 TABLESPOON	*kosher salt*
2 TEASPOONS	*freshly ground black pepper*
4 CUPS	*medium-diced carrots (6 to 8 carrots)*
2 CUPS	*medium-diced red boiling potatoes, unpeeled (6 small)*
2 POUNDS	*dried split green peas*
16 CUPS	*chicken stock or water*

Kosher salt is "softer" or sweeter than iodized salt, and most restaurant chefs prefer it.

Split pea soup will thicken considerably when it sits. Adjust the consistency by adding more stock or water.

In an 8-quart stockpot on medium heat, sauté the onions and garlic with the olive oil, oregano, salt, and pepper until the onions are translucent, 10 to 15 minutes. Add the carrots, potatoes, 1½ pounds of split peas, and chicken stock. Bring to a boil, then simmer uncovered for 40 minutes. Skim off the foam while cooking. Add the remaining split peas and continue to simmer for another 40 minutes, or until all the peas are soft. Stir frequently to keep the solids from burning on the bottom. Taste for salt and pepper. Serve hot.

cheddar corn chowder

SERVES 10 TO 12

This hearty soup tastes more like stew. Fresh corn is sweetest in August and September, but since I love this soup all winter, I've been known to cheat and use frozen corn. The flavor is not exactly the same, but it is still a great lunch. This is one of the most popular soups we make in the store.

8 OUNCES	*bacon, chopped*
¼ CUP	*good olive oil*
6 CUPS	*chopped yellow onions (4 large onions)*
4 TABLESPOONS	*unsalted butter*
½ CUP	*all-purpose flour*
2 TEASPOONS	*kosher salt*
1 TEASPOON	*freshly ground black pepper*
½ TEASPOON	*ground turmeric*
12 CUPS	*chicken stock*
6 CUPS	*medium-diced white boiling potatoes, unpeeled (2 pounds)*
10 CUPS	*corn kernels, fresh (10 ears) or frozen (3 pounds)*
2 CUPS	*half-and-half*
½ POUND	*sharp white Cheddar cheese, grated*

Unpeeled potatoes are easier to use and give this soup an earthy flavor.

In a large stockpot on medium-high heat, cook the bacon and olive oil until the bacon is crisp, about 5 minutes. Remove the bacon with a slotted spoon and reserve. Reduce the heat to medium, add the onions and butter to the fat, and cook for 10 minutes, until the onions are translucent.

Stir in the flour, salt, pepper, and turmeric and cook for

3 minutes. Add the chicken stock and potatoes, bring to a boil, and simmer uncovered for 15 minutes, until the potatoes are tender. If using fresh corn, cut the kernels off the cobs and blanch the kernels for 3 minutes in boiling salted water. Drain. (If using frozen corn, you can skip this step.) Add the corn to the soup, then add the half-and-half and Cheddar. Cook for 5 more minutes, until the cheese is melted. Season to taste with salt and pepper. Serve hot with a garnish of bacon.

french onion soup

SERVES 4 TO 6

Paul Hodges is a wonderful cook and he makes this soup at Barefoot Contessa. Beef and veal stocks make this a truly extraordinary soup, but you can substitute chicken stock if you're in a hurry. Serve this soup with Parmesan Croutons (page 87) and lots of grated Parmesan cheese.

2½ POUNDS	*yellow onions, halved, and sliced ¼ inch thick (8 cups)*
¼ POUND	*unsalted butter*
1	*bay leaf*
½ CUP	*medium-dry sherry*
½ CUP	*brandy or Cognac*
1½ CUPS	*good dry white wine*
4 CUPS	*beef stock*
4 CUPS	*veal stock*
1 TABLESPOON	*kosher salt*
½ TEASPOON	*freshly ground white pepper*
	Freshly grated Parmesan cheese

I like to use large Spanish onions; they're sweeter and much easier to slice than small yellow ones.

In a large stockpot on medium-high heat, sauté the onions with the butter and bay leaf for 20 minutes, until the onions turn a rich golden brown color. Deglaze the pan with the sherry and brandy and simmer uncovered for 5 minutes. Add the white wine and simmer uncovered for 15 more minutes.

Add the beef and veal stocks plus salt and pepper. Bring to a boil, then simmer uncovered for 20 minutes. Remove the bay leaf, taste for salt and pepper, and serve hot with grated Parmesan cheese.

roasted-potato fennel soup

SERVES 10 TO 12

I love to make this soup in the dead of winter when just about all you can find are potatoes and fennel. The potatoes are roasted first to give them extra flavor, and I add a touch of heavy cream at the end to give the soup a little richness.

4 POUNDS	*red potatoes, unpeeled and quartered*
¼ CUP	*plus 2 tablespoons good olive oil*
1 TABLESPOON	*minced garlic (3 cloves)*
1 TABLESPOON	*kosher salt*
2 TEASPOONS	*freshly ground black pepper*
4 CUPS	*chopped yellow onions (4 onions)*
4 CUPS	*chopped fennel bulb (about 2 pounds)*
3 QUARTS	*chicken stock or water*
1 CUP	*heavy cream*

Leaving the potatoes unpeeled makes this a very easy soup and gives it an earthy flavor and texture.

Preheat the oven to 400 degrees.

In a large bowl, toss the potatoes with ¼ cup olive oil, garlic, salt, and pepper. Spread on a baking sheet and roast for 30 minutes, until cooked through.

Sauté the onions and fennel with 2 tablespoons olive oil in a large stockpot on medium heat until translucent, 10 to 15 minutes. Add the roasted potatoes (including the scrapings from the pan) and the chicken stock. Cover and bring to a boil. Lower the heat and simmer uncovered for 1 hour, until all of the vegetables are very soft. Add the heavy cream and allow the soup to cool slightly. Pass the soup through the largest disk of a food mill or chop coarsely in batches in a food processor fitted with a metal blade. Taste for salt and pepper. Reheat and serve hot.

gazpacho

SERVES 8 TO 10

The silliest question I've ever been asked at Barefoot Contessa was "Do you have any gestapo?" I feel very strongly about gazpacho. For me, it should be chunky and spicy, but not hot, and never puréed or it will taste like V-8 in a bowl. To get just the right texture, we chop each vegetable separately in a food processor. In the summer, this feels like the healthiest lunch in the world. Try Parmesan Croutons (page 87) on top!

2	*hothouse cucumbers,*
	halved and seeded, but not peeled
3	*red bell peppers, cored and seeded*
8	*plum tomatoes*
2	*red onions*
6	*garlic cloves, minced*
46 OUNCES	*tomato juice (6 cups)*
½ CUP	*white wine vinegar*
½ CUP	*good olive oil*
1 TABLESPOON	*kosher salt*
1½ TEASPOONS	*freshly ground black pepper*

Roughly chop the cucumbers, bell peppers, tomatoes, and red onions into 1-inch cubes. Put each vegetable separately into a food processor fitted with a steel blade and pulse until it is coarsely chopped. Do not overprocess!

After each vegetable is processed, combine them in a large bowl and add the garlic, tomato juice, vinegar, olive oil, salt, and pepper. Mix well and chill before serving. The longer gazpacho sits, the more the flavors develop.

Hothouse (English or seedless) cucumbers are the long thin ones usually sold individually wrapped. Not only do they have fewer seeds, but the flavor is much sweeter than traditional cucumbers.

Sacramento tomato juice has the most flavor of any brand, and it makes a tremendous difference in the flavor of the gazpacho.

lentil vegetable soup

SERVES 8 TO 10

This is a delicious and hearty winter soup that gets a lot of its flavor and texture from French lentils. They are the small green ones that are available from specialty food stores or by mail order. French lentils make this soup taste fresher and less starchy than the traditional American ones.

1 POUND	*French green lentils*
4 CUPS	*chopped yellow onions (3 large onions)*
4 CUPS	*chopped leeks, white part only (2 leeks)*
1 TABLESPOON	*minced garlic (3 cloves)*
¼ CUP	*good olive oil, plus additional for drizzling on top*
1 TABLESPOON	*kosher salt*
1½ TEASPOONS	*freshly ground black pepper*
1 TABLESPOON	*minced fresh thyme leaves or 1 teaspoon dried*
1 TEASPOON	*ground cumin*
3 CUPS	*medium-diced celery (8 stalks)*
3 CUPS	*medium-diced carrots (4 to 6 carrots)*
3 QUARTS	*chicken stock*
¼ CUP	*tomato paste*
2 TABLESPOONS	*red wine or red wine vinegar*
	Freshly grated Parmesan cheese

As lentil soup sits, it will thicken; just add more chicken stock to get the right consistency.

Red wine vinegars vary greatly in strength. Put half the vinegar into the soup, taste it, and then add the rest if you want more. Williams-Sonoma (page 249) has a very good but strong Napa Valley Cabernet Sauvignon red wine vinegar.

In a large bowl, cover the lentils with boiling water and allow to sit for 15 minutes. Drain.

In a large stockpot on medium heat, sauté the onions, leeks, and garlic with the olive oil, salt, pepper, thyme, and cumin for 20 minutes, until the vegetables are translucent and very tender. Add the celery and carrots and sauté for 10 more minutes. Add the chicken stock, tomato paste, and lentils. Cover and bring to a boil. Reduce the heat and simmer uncovered for one hour, until the lentils are cooked through. Check the seasonings. Add the red wine and serve hot, drizzled with olive oil and sprinkled with grated Parmesan.

rosemary white bean soup

SERVES 6

This soup is as simple and satisfying as any soup we do and always reminds me of Tuscany. Fresh rosemary is truly essential.

1 POUND	*dried white cannellini beans*
4 CUPS	*sliced yellow onions (3 onions)*
¼ CUP	*good olive oil*
2	*garlic cloves, minced*
1	*large branch fresh rosemary (6 to 7 inches)*
2 QUARTS	*chicken stock*
1	*bay leaf*
2 TEASPOONS	*kosher salt*
½ TEASPOON	*freshly ground black pepper*

In a medium bowl, cover the beans with water by at least 1 inch and leave them in the refrigerator for 6 hours or overnight. Drain.

In a large stockpot over low to medium heat, sauté the onions with the olive oil until the onions are translucent, 10 to 15 minutes. Add the garlic and cook over low heat for 3 more minutes. Add the drained white beans, rosemary, chicken stock, and bay leaf. Cover, bring to a boil, and simmer for 30 to 40 minutes, until the beans are very soft. Remove the rosemary branch and the bay leaf. Pass the soup through the coarsest blade of a food mill, or place in the bowl of a food processor fitted with a steel blade and pulse until coarsely puréed. Return the soup to the pot to reheat and add salt and pepper to taste. Serve hot.

If you add salt before the beans are cooked, they become tough.

Dried white cannellini beans can be found in Italian and specialty food stores or by mail order.

roasted-tomato basil soup

SERVES 6 TO 8

*This is it: the perfect tomato soup. It is delicious all year 'round because
roasting the tomatoes gives them a rich "summer" tomato flavor.*

3 POUNDS	*ripe plum tomatoes, cut in half lengthwise*
¼ CUP	*plus 2 tablespoons good olive oil*
1 TABLESPOON	*kosher salt*
1½ TEASPOONS	*freshly ground black pepper*
2 CUPS	*chopped yellow onions (2 onions)*
6	*garlic cloves, minced*
2 TABLESPOONS	*unsalted butter*
¼ TEASPOON	*crushed red pepper flakes*
28 OUNCES	*canned plum tomatoes with their juice*
4 CUPS	*fresh basil leaves, packed*
1 TEASPOON	*fresh thyme leaves*
1 QUART	*chicken stock or water*

*I serve this soup
hot with a chiffonade
of fresh basil leaves, or
cold with a dollop of
crème fraîche.*

Preheat the oven to 400 degrees.

Toss together the tomatoes, ¼ cup olive oil, salt, and pepper.
Spread the tomatoes in one layer on a baking sheet and roast for
45 minutes.

In an 8-quart stockpot on medium heat, sauté the onions and
garlic with 2 tablespoons of olive oil, butter, and red pepper flakes
for 10 minutes, until the onions start to brown. Add the canned
tomatoes, basil, thyme, and chicken stock. Add the oven-roasted
tomatoes, including the liquid on the baking sheet. Bring to a boil
and simmer uncovered for 40 minutes. Pass through a food mill fitted with the coarsest blade. Taste the seasonings. Serve hot or cold.

parmesan croutons

MAKES 20 TO 25 CROUTONS

At Barefoot Contessa, we devised this recipe to use leftover baguettes, but they were so popular, we immediately had to start baking more breads! In the store, we call them Parmesan Toasts because they are delicious as crackers for appetizers, but here I call them Parmesan Croutons because I love them on top of Gazpacho (page 79) and Lentil Vegetable Soup (page 80). They are also a great snack, so be sure to make a lot!

1	*baguette*
¼ CUP	*good olive oil, plain or flavored with basil or garlic*
	Kosher salt
	Freshly ground black pepper
¾ CUP	*freshly shredded Parmesan cheese (3 ounces)*

Preheat the oven to 400 degrees.

Slice the baguette diagonally into ¼-inch-thick slices. Depending on the size of the baguette, you should get about 20 to 25 slices.

Lay the slices in one layer on a baking sheet and brush each with olive oil and sprinkle liberally with salt and pepper. Sprinkle with shredded Parmesan. Bake the toasts for 15 to 20 minutes, until they are browned and crisp. Serve at room temperature.

I prefer the Parmesan grated as you would grate carrots, rather than the more traditional "grated" Parmesan, which is actually finely ground.

There are several grades of Italian Parmesan cheese. I always use Reggiano, which is considered the finest, and I try to find one that has been aged at least two years.

salads

Beets with Orange Vinaigrette

Curried Couscous

French Potato Salad

Provençal Potato Salad

Grilled Lemon Chicken Salad

Broccoli with Garlic

Fresh Corn Salad

Grilled Salmon Salad

Sugar Snap Peas with Sesame

Vegetable Coleslaw

Szechuan Noodles

Crudité Platter

creating a salad

Many years ago, I read an article by Craig Claiborne in which he said his most frequently asked question was "How do you make up a recipe?" He replied that recipes evolve. If I remember correctly, he then went on to show how spaghetti and meatballs, which was popular twenty years ago, changed to pasta primavera.

Salads are a perfect place to start inventing recipes. They are easy to fix when they go wrong. When you're baking a cake, you don't know there's too much salt until the cake is out of the oven. With salads, you can usually fix a problem by adding another ingredient; or you can sometimes just take one out.

Let's take grilled salmon salad. Since we are near the ocean, I wanted to make a new fish salad for the store. The "old-fashioned" version is, of course, tuna salad. But there is no fresh taste, so I decided to start with fresh fish. Fresh tuna can be temperamental, so I made the salad with fresh salmon, which stays moist, tastes wonderful, and makes a beautiful salad. Rather than poaching it, I got the most flavor by grilling the fish and then breaking it up into large flakes. Then I chose vegetables and herbs that would add to the flavor rather than overwhelm it.

The sauce was next. An "old-fashioned" sauce is made with a mayonnaise and added flavorings. But the fish and vegetables were so colorful and light that I wanted to make a vinaigrette to complement the fish, not mask it, so I chose raspberry vinegar and olive oil. I tossed it all together and made one of my favorite salads of all time.

The recipes that follow are on the menu at Barefoot Contessa and you can make them easily at home. But be creative and let new ingredients and flavors evolve so you can make salads that will surprise you.

beets with orange vinaigrette

SERVES 6–8

This recipe is not only okay to make ahead, it actually tastes better *if it is allowed to sit in the refrigerator for a few days while the vinaigrette soaks into the beets. If you are in a hurry, use canned baby beets.*

3 POUNDS	*fresh beets (3 bunches) or*
	3 15-ounce cans of baby beets, drained
2 TABLESPOONS	*raspberry vinegar*
2 TABLESPOONS	*freshly squeezed orange juice*
3 TABLESPOONS	*good olive oil*
1/2 TEASPOON	*sugar*
1 1/2 TEASPOONS	*kosher salt*
1/2 TEASPOON	*freshly ground black pepper*
1/2 CUP	*small-diced red onion (1 small onion)*
	Zest of 2 large navel oranges
	Segments of 2 large navel oranges

I like to zest the oranges and cut out the orange segments directly over the bowl of beets to catch all the oil from the zest and the juice from the oranges.

Beets are sweetest in late summer and early autumn.

If you are using fresh beets, trim off the green tops and place the beets in a large pot of salted water to cover. Bring to a boil and simmer uncovered for 50 minutes to 1 hour, until the beets are just tender. Drain and allow to sit until cool enough to handle.

Peel and dice the beets into 1/2-inch cubes. (If using canned beets, drain the liquid and dice the beets into 1/2-inch cubes.) While the beets are still warm, place them in a mixing bowl and add the raspberry vinegar, orange juice, olive oil, sugar, salt, pepper, red onions, orange zest, and orange segments. Mix well, taste for salt and pepper, and serve cold or at room temperature.

curried couscous

SERVES 6

This dish may have lots of ingredients, but it doesn't feel like cooking, so I love to make it. It is literally as easy as boiling water. I actually make it with different vegetables each time, sometimes just looking in the pantry for inspiration. That's when the best surprises happen. If you don't have dried currants, use golden raisins or dried cranberries. This is a terrific side dish for chicken or lamb.

Curry powder is a combination of spices and varies greatly by producer. I experiment to find the mixture that has depth of flavor, sweetness, and just a little heat.

1½ CUPS	*couscous*
1 TABLESPOON	*unsalted butter*
1½ CUPS	*boiling water*
¼ CUP	*plain yogurt*
¼ CUP	*good olive oil*
1 TEASPOON	*white wine vinegar*
1 TEASPOON	*curry powder*
¼ TEASPOON	*ground turmeric*
1½ TEASPOONS	*kosher salt*
1 TEASPOON	*freshly ground black pepper*
½ CUP	*grated (or small-diced) carrots*
½ CUP	*minced fresh-flat leaf parsley*
½ CUP	*dried currants*
¼ CUP	*blanched, sliced almonds*
2	*scallions, thinly sliced (white and green parts)*
¼ CUP	*small-diced red onion*

Place the couscous in a medium bowl. Melt the butter in the boiling water and pour over the couscous. Cover tightly and allow the couscous to soak for 5 minutes. Fluff with a fork.

Whisk together the yogurt, olive oil, vinegar, curry, turmeric, salt, and pepper. Pour over the fluffed couscous and mix well with a fork. Add the carrots, parsley, currants, almonds, scallions, and red onions; mix well and taste for seasonings. Serve at room temperature.

french potato salad

SERVES 4 TO 6

Everyone made American potato salad with mayonnaise until Julia Child showed us how to appreciate the freshness and beauty of perfectly cooked potatoes with green herbs and a flavorful vinaigrette. This is my version of her dish. It is most delicious in early autumn when the small potatoes have been freshly dug and they have a sweet flavor and a creamy texture. I also love to make it into a beautiful summer lunch by adding all kinds of delicious Provençal ingredients (see the Provençal Potato Salad, page 98).

1 POUND	*small white boiling potatoes*
1 POUND	*small red boiling potatoes*
2 TABLESPOONS	*good dry white wine*
2 TABLESPOONS	*chicken stock*
3 TABLESPOONS	*champagne vinegar*
1/2 TEASPOON	*Dijon mustard*
2 TEASPOONS	*kosher salt*
3/4 TEASPOON	*freshly ground black pepper*
10 TABLESPOONS	*good olive oil*
1/4 CUP	*minced scallions (white and green parts)*
2 TABLESPOONS	*minced fresh dill*
2 TABLESPOONS	*minced flat-leaf parsley*
2 TABLESPOONS	*chiffonade of fresh basil leaves*

Choose white and red potatoes of similar sizes so they cook for the same length of time.

Drop the white and red potatoes into a large pot of boiling salted water and cook for 20 to 30 minutes, until they are just cooked through. Drain in a colander and place a towel over the potatoes to allow them to steam for 10 more minutes. As soon as you can handle them, cut in half (quarters if the potatoes are larger) and place in a medium bowl. Toss gently with the wine and chicken stock. Allow the liquids to soak into the warm potatoes before proceeding.

Combine the vinegar, mustard, $\frac{1}{2}$ teaspoon salt, and $\frac{1}{4}$ teaspoon pepper and slowly whisk in the olive oil to make an emulsion. Add the vinaigrette to the potatoes. Add the scallions, dill, parsley, basil, $1\frac{1}{2}$ teaspoons salt, and $\frac{1}{2}$ teaspoon pepper and toss. Serve warm or at room temperature.

provençal potato salad

SERVES 6

This is a wonderful summer afternoon lunch. It is a breeze to prepare and requires no last-minute cooking to serve for a party. In fact, it tastes better if it has an hour or so to sit for the flavors to soak into the potatoes.

½ POUND	*haricots verts, stems removed*
1 RECIPE	*French Potato Salad (page 96)*
1	*6-ounce can Italian tuna, drained and flaked*
½ CUP	*capers, drained*
1 CUP	*halved cherry tomatoes*
½ CUP	*small-diced red onion (1 small onion)*
½ CUP	*good black olives, pitted*
6	*hard-cooked eggs, peeled and quartered (optional)*
6	*anchovy fillets (optional)*

In a pot of boiling salted water, blanch the haricots verts for 3 to 5 minutes, until barely tender. Drain and immerse into ice water for 5 minutes. Drain again.

In a large bowl, combine the haricots verts with the potato salad, tuna, capers, tomatoes, onions, olives, eggs, and anchovy fillets. Serve at room temperature.

To make hard-cooked eggs with no darkness around the yolks, put the eggs in a pan, cover with cold water, and bring to a full boil. Turn off the heat and allow them to sit for 5 minutes. Remove the eggs from the water, cool for 2 minutes, and peel.

"Shocking" the haricots verts in ice water immediately after blanching will ensure they stay bright green and crisp.

Italian canned tuna is moister and more flavorful than American tuna.

grilled lemon chicken salad

SERVES 6

This recipe was developed on the spur of the moment: I needed a salad idea quickly and I looked around the refrigerator to see what was available. Grilled lemon chicken, sugar snap peas, and fresh bell peppers with a lemon vinaigrette turned out to be the most popular salad of all times, and we've been making it ever since. In the spring, I sometimes substitute thin, blanched fresh asparagus for the sugar snap peas.

2 POUNDS	*Grilled Lemon Chicken (page 48)*
¼ CUP	*freshly squeezed lemon juice (1 large lemon)*
¼ CUP	*good olive oil*
1 CUP	*raw sugar snap peas, stems and strings removed*
½	*red bell pepper, julienned*
½	*yellow bell pepper, julienned*
1	*lemon, thinly sliced*
¼ TEASPOON	*kosher salt*
¼ TEASPOON	*freshly ground black pepper*

Freshly squeezed lemon juice is essential to the flavor of this salad.

I like a salad to look like what it is: using lemon slices in the salad complements the lemon vinaigrette.

After the chicken is grilled, chill it in the refrigerator. Slice the breasts diagonally into ⅜-inch-thick slices. Toss them in a bowl with their juices plus the lemon juice, olive oil, sugar snap peas, red and yellow bell peppers, lemon slices, salt, and pepper.

Taste for seasonings and serve cold or at room temperature.

broccoli with garlic

SERVES 6 TO 8

Sometimes the most popular salad is the simplest. The garlic can be cooked ahead of time and stored for weeks in your refrigerator.

1 HEAD *garlic, peeled (about 16 cloves)*
1 CUP *good olive oil*
1 TEASPOON *crushed red pepper flakes*
1 TEASPOON *kosher salt*
4 STALKS *broccoli, cut into florets (8 cups of florets)*

I like to cut the broccoli so there's an inch of stalk, but you may prefer to use only the florets.

Put the garlic cloves and oil in a small heavy-bottomed saucepan. Bring to a boil and cook uncovered over low heat for 10 to 15 minutes, until the garlic is browned and tender. Turn off the heat and add the red pepper flakes and $1/2$ teaspoon salt. Immediately pour into a heat-proof container to stop the cooking. Allow to cool to room temperature.

For the salad, blanch the broccoli florets in a large pot of boiling salted water for 2 to 3 minutes, until crisp-tender. Drain well and immerse immediately into a large bowl of ice water until the broccoli is cooled. This process stops the cooking and sets the bright green color. Drain well.

In a large bowl, toss the broccoli with $1/2$ teaspoon salt, $1/4$ cup of the oil used to cook the garlic, and 8 or more cloves of cooked garlic. Taste for seasonings and serve cold or at room temperature.

fresh corn salad

SERVES 4 TO 6

Since many of the local farmers in East Hampton have grown corn for generations, corn is a staple here. I can't wait for the first crop to hit the farm stands so I can make our fresh corn salad. Neither can our customers. July and August are peak season, but I also find the corn very sweet through September. For a particularly beautiful salad, you can mix white and yellow corn.

5 EARS	*corn, shucked*
½ CUP	*small-diced red onion*
	(1 small onion)
3 TABLESPOONS	*cider vinegar*
3 TABLESPOONS	*good olive oil*
½ TEASPOON	*kosher salt*
½ TEASPOON	*freshly ground black pepper*
½ CUP	*chiffonade fresh basil leaves*

In a large pot of boiling salted water, cook the corn for 3 minutes until the starchiness is just gone. Drain and immerse it in ice water to stop the cooking and to set the color. When the corn is cool, cut the kernels off the cob, cutting close to the cob.

Toss the kernels in a large bowl with the red onions, vinegar, olive oil, salt, and pepper. Just before serving, toss in the fresh basil. Taste for seasonings and serve cold or at room temperature.

Don't substitute frozen corn; it doesn't have the texture or flavor you want in a fresh salad.

grilled salmon salad

SERVES 4

*Most salad recipes require making the salad first and then the vinai-
grette. At Barefoot Contessa we often just toss all the ingredients together
and get the same delicious flavor with less work and fewer bowls. And
sometimes the result is even magical, like the combination of grilled
salmon and raspberry vinegar.*

2 POUNDS	*fresh salmon fillets, with the skin on*
	Good olive oil, for grilling
	Kosher salt
	Freshly ground black pepper
1 CUP	*small-diced celery (3 stalks)*
½ CUP	*small-diced red onion (1 small onion)*
2 TABLESPOONS	*minced fresh dill*
2 TABLESPOONS	*capers, drained*
2 TABLESPOONS	*raspberry vinegar*
2 TABLESPOONS	*good olive oil*
½ TEASPOON	*kosher salt*
½ TEASPOON	*freshly ground black pepper*

Prepare the grill with hot coals.

Cut the salmon fillets crosswise into 4-inch-wide slices. Rub
them with olive oil and sprinkle with salt and pepper. Brush the
cooking surface with oil to prevent the fish from sticking. Cook
the fillets on the grill for 5 to 7 minutes on each side, until they
are rare. Be sure they are still rare on the inside. Remove to a
plate, wrap with plastic, and chill in the refrigerator until cold
and very firm.

When the fillets are cold, remove any skin that hasn't come off during grilling. Break the fillets into very large flakes and put them into a bowl, adding any juice that has collected at the bottom of the plate.

Add the celery, red onions, dill, capers, raspberry vinegar, olive oil, salt, and pepper to taste. Mix well and serve cold or at room temperature.

sugar snap peas with sesame

SERVES 5 TO 6

Sometimes a mistake turns out to be a blessing. Years ago, I ordered snow peas from my produce supplier, who accidentally sent sugar snap peas, which were new on the market. While I was on the phone telling the supplier to pick them up, I tasted one. They were delicious! So, on the spot, I asked the cooks to add sesame oil and black sesame seeds, to see if customers would like them. An hour later, I called the supplier back and ordered 100 pounds for the next day. Fifteen years later, this is still one of our best sellers. And nothing could be easier to make at home.

> 1 POUND *fresh sugar snap peas*
> *Dark sesame oil*
> *Black sesame seeds*

Pick through the sugar snap peas to remove any that aren't perfect. Remove and discard the stem end and the string from each pod. Toss the sugar snap peas in a bowl with sesame oil and sesame seeds to taste. Serve at room temperature.

Black sesame seeds are available from Asian groceries and specialty food stores.

Sugar snap peas are in season during June in the Northeast, but they are available from California almost all year long.

vegetable coleslaw

SERVES 8 TO 10

This coleslaw is a Barefoot Contessa classic. It is like traditional coleslaw, but has a lot more flavor. The vegetables can be sliced by hand, but I find it's faster to use a food processor.

1 POUND	*white cabbage ($^1\!/_2$ small head)*
¾ POUND	*red cabbage ($^1\!/_2$ small head)*
5	*carrots*
2 CUPS	*good mayonnaise*
¼ CUP	*Dijon mustard*
1 TABLESPOON	*sugar*
2 TABLESPOONS	*cider vinegar*
2 TEASPOONS	*celery seeds*
1 TEASPOON	*celery salt*
½ TEASPOON	*kosher salt*
½ TEASPOON	*freshly ground black pepper*

Placing the vegetables horizontally in the food processor ensures long shreds.

The vegetables can be grated a day ahead and stored, wrapped in plastic, in the refrigerator. Keep the red cabbage separate, or it will turn the other vegetables pink.

Fit a food processor with the thickest slicing blade. Cut the cabbages into small wedges and place horizontally into the feed tube. Process in batches. Next, fit the food processor with the grating blade. Cut the carrots in half and place in the feed tube so they are lying on their sides. Process in batches and mix in a bowl with the grated cabbages.

In a medium bowl, whisk together the mayonnaise, mustard, sugar, vinegar, celery seeds, celery salt, salt, and pepper. Pour enough of the dressing over the grated vegetables to moisten them. Serve cold or at room temperature.

szechuan noodles

I love the complex flavor of this salad. Almost all the ingredients can be stored in the pantry, so it requires very little last-minute shopping. The sauce can actually be made a week ahead and then added to the hot cooked pasta just before serving.

6	*garlic cloves, chopped*
¼ CUP	*fresh ginger, peeled and chopped*
½ CUP	*vegetable oil*
½ CUP	*tahini (sesame paste)*
½ CUP	*smooth peanut butter*
½ CUP	*good soy sauce*
¼ CUP	*dry sherry*
¼ CUP	*sherry vinegar*
¼ CUP	*honey*
½ TEASPOON	*hot chili oil*
2 TABLESPOONS	*dark sesame oil*
½ TEASPOON	*freshly ground black pepper*
⅛ TEASPOON	*ground cayenne pepper*
1 POUND	*spaghetti*
1	*red bell pepper, julienned*
1	*yellow bell pepper, julienned*
4	*scallions, sliced diagonally (white and green parts)*

Place the garlic and ginger in a food processor fitted with a steel blade. Add the vegetable oil, tahini, peanut butter, soy sauce, sherry, sherry vinegar, honey, chili oil, sesame oil, and ground peppers. Purée the sauce.

Add a splash of oil to a large pot of boiling salted water and cook the spaghetti al dente. Drain the pasta in a colander, place it in a large bowl, and while still warm, toss with three-quarters of the sauce. Add the red and yellow bell peppers and scallions; toss well. Serve warm or at room temperature. The remaining sauce may be added, as needed, to moisten the pasta.

Don't combine the sauce with the pasta until the last minute; the soy sauce tends to break down the noodles and make them mushy.

crudité platter

In the United States, we think of crudité as a basket of fresh vegetables to eat with a dip at cocktail time. In France, crudité is an assortment of raw vegetables and it is served as a salad with a vinaigrette. I love to make this kind of salad because it can require no cooking, plus it looks gorgeous when you bring it to the table. This platter will serve 6 people.

1 LARGE BUNCH	*arugula, stems removed*
1 LARGE HEAD	*radicchio, cut into wedges*
2 HEADS	*Belgian endive, cut lengthwise into quarters*
3	*baby red carrots, cut in half lengthwise*
3	*scallions, whole*
1 BULB	*fennel, sliced very thinly*
1 BUNCH	*radishes, whole, with tops*

These are the kinds of fresh vegetables and salad "greens"
you can use:

Carrots, grated or julienned   *Cherry tomatoes*

Fennel, shredded or cut into wedges   *Tomatoes, sliced*

Belgian endive, sliced lengthwise   *Haricots verts, blanched*

Radishes, whole or thinly sliced   *Celeriac, julienned*

Radicchio, shredded or cut into wedges *Jicama, julienned*

Bell peppers, julienned   *Sugar snap peas*

Watercress   *Snow peas*

Arugula

Jim Pike's farmstand.

¼ CUP *freshly squeezed lemon juice (1 large lemon)*

½ CUP *good olive oil*

½ TEASPOON *kosher salt*

¼ TEASPOON *freshly ground black pepper*

Parmesan cheese

Arrange the salad ingredients beautifully on a platter. Whisk
together the lemon juice, olive oil, salt, and pepper. Serve the
vinaigrette on the side in a carafe or small pitcher. You can also
put a chunk of Parmesan cheese on a plate with a vegetable
peeler or cheese grater for guests to help themselves.

dinner

Baked Virginia Ham

Barbecued Chicken
   with Barbecue Sauce

Filet of Beef Bourguignon

Indonesian Ginger Chicken

Kitchen Clambake

Lemon Capellini with Caviar

Perfect Roast Chicken

Lobster Potpie

Salmon with Fennel

Swordfish with Tomatoes
   and Capers

Turkey Meat Loaf

Grilled Tuna Niçoise Platter

come for dinner

Dinner parties can be really fun or deadly boring. I have been a caterer for twenty years and, believe me, I've seen all the possibilities. Over the years, I've developed a few secrets to a successful dinner party. A good party starts with the right number of people: 4 to 8 are ideal, or 10 to 12 for a more festive celebration. I find it's easier to keep everyone involved in the conversation with a smaller group. The next thing is the size of the table; a table that's a little too small makes a more intimate party and creates energy. Even if I have a party at a restaurant, I will go there the day before to make sure the table is the right size. It's often the difference between a fun, lively party and one that's quiet and awkward.

The right seating plan can make a good party better. With a rectangular table, I put the most outgoing talkers in the middle, facing each other. This keeps the party from fracturing into two groups at opposite ends of the table.

Next, make the meal very simple. If you are jumping up and down to change plates or to finish the cooking, your guests will feel awkward. My friend Suzanna Guiliano actually arranges the whole dinner before guests arrive, including vegetables, on an ironstone platter and keeps it warm in the oven until everyone sits down. Then she takes the platter from the oven and puts it in the center of the table, and the guests help themselves family style. What could be more relaxed?

Finally, the best parties I give have an element of surprise. When my husband was an investment banker, his friends were more formal and expected fancy dinner parties. Instead, I would serve "hands-on" food like a clambake or barbecued chicken and cornbread. People rolled up their sleeves and dug in. And they always had a great time.

baked virginia ham

SERVES 35 FOR DINNER, 50 FOR COCKTAILS
This is the ultimate holiday party dish. The glaze takes only a minute to make and the ham tastes like you worked for hours. We order a "spiral-cut" smoked ham from the butcher, so we don't even have to slice it! How lazy is that? I like to serve it for cocktails with mini corn muffins or for dinner with extra mustard and chutney.

Choose the best quality ham you can find, and either buy a "spiral-cut" ham, or have the butcher slice and retie a whole smoked ham.

1 (14- TO 16-POUND)	*fully cooked, spiral-cut smoked ham*
6	*garlic cloves*
8½ OUNCES	*mango chutney*
½ CUP	*Dijon mustard*
1 CUP	*light brown sugar, packed*
	Zest of 1 orange
¼ CUP	*freshly squeezed orange juice*

We use Major Grey's chutney.

Preheat the oven to 350 degrees. Place the ham in a heavy roasting pan.

Mince the garlic in a food processor fitted with the steel blade. Add the chutney, mustard, brown sugar, orange zest, and orange juice and process until smooth. Pour the glaze over the ham and bake for 1 hour, until the ham is fully heated and the glaze is well browned. Serve hot or at room temperature.

barbecued chicken

SERVES 6

Why doesn't it feel like a barbecue until the meat catches on fire? I use a charcoal chimney to start the fire and then I distribute the coals to make a low, even heat. Chicken needs to cook for at least forty-five minutes, so you want to grill it slowly. Flare-ups from the drips will give enough charcoal flavor to make the chicken taste great. You can do this with any barbecue sauce.

2 chickens (2^1/$_2$ to 3 pounds each),
quartered, with backs removed
1 RECIPE *Barbecue Sauce (recipe follows)*

Heat the coals in a charcoal grill.

Marinate the chickens in two-thirds of the barbecue sauce for a few hours or overnight in the refrigerator. Spread the bottom of the grill with a single layer of hot coals and then add a few more coals 5 minutes before cooking, which will keep the fire going longer. Place the chicken quarters on the grill, skin side down, and cook for about 45 minutes, turning once or twice to cook evenly on both sides. Brush with the marinade as needed. The chicken quarters are done when you insert a knife between a leg and thigh and the juices run clear.

Serve with extra barbecue sauce on the side.

Never use leftover marinade to serve with the cooked chicken. The marinade may contain uncooked salmonella bacteria, which is very dangerous. Use fresh sauce on the side.

barbecue sauce

MAKES 1½ QUARTS

This is a famous Barefoot Contessa recipe. It has a lot of ingredients, but it's easy to make and lasts for months in the refrigerator.

1½ CUPS	*chopped yellow onion (1 large onion)*
1 TABLESPOON	*minced garlic (3 cloves)*
½ CUP	*vegetable oil*
1 CUP	*tomato paste (10 ounces)*
1 CUP	*cider vinegar*
1 CUP	*honey*
½ CUP	*Worcestershire sauce*
1 CUP	*Dijon mustard*
½ CUP	*soy sauce*
1 CUP	*hoisin sauce*
2 TABLESPOONS	*chili powder*
1 TABLESPOON	*ground cumin*
½ TABLESPOON	*crushed red pepper flakes*

In a large saucepan on low heat, sauté the onions and garlic with the vegetable oil for 10 to 15 minutes, until the onions are translucent but not browned. Add the tomato paste, vinegar, honey, Worcestershire sauce, mustard, soy sauce, hoisin sauce, chili powder, cumin, and red pepper flakes. Simmer uncovered on low heat for 30 minutes. Use immediately or store in the refrigerator.

filet of beef bourguignon

SERVES 6 TO 8

I love to update classic recipes. Twenty years ago, I used to follow Julia Child's wonderful beef bourguignon recipe, but stewing beef can take a very long time, so I decided to make a version based on quickly sautéed filets of beef. It cooks in a quarter of the time and I think it is fresher than the original. This dish tastes even better the second day, so you can make it ahead and reheat it before dinner.

1 3-POUND	*filet of beef, trimmed*
	Kosher salt
	Freshly ground black pepper
3 TO 4 TABLESPOONS	*good olive oil*
¼ POUND	*bacon, diced*
2	*garlic cloves, minced*
1½ CUPS	*good dry red wine, such as*
	Burgundy or Chianti
2 CUPS	*beef stock*
1 TABLESPOON	*tomato paste*
1 SPRIG	*fresh thyme*
½ POUND	*pearl onions, peeled*
8 TO 10	*carrots, cut diagonally into 1-inch-thick slices*
3 TABLESPOONS	*unsalted butter at room temperature*
2 TABLESPOONS	*all-purpose flour*
½ POUND	*mushrooms, sliced ¼-inch thick*
	(domestic or wild)

This dish is excellent made in advance and refrigerated in the pan. When you are ready to serve, heat the filets and sauce over low heat for 10 to 15 minutes, until heated through.

To peel the pearl onions easily, first blanch them for a minute or two in boiling water.

continued next page

With a sharp knife, cut the filet crosswise into 1-inch-thick slices. Salt and pepper the filets on both sides. In a large, heavy-bottomed pan on medium-high heat, sauté the slices of beef in batches with 2 to 3 tablespoons oil until browned on the outside and very rare inside, about 2 to 3 minutes on each side. Remove the filets from the pan and set aside on a platter.

In the same pan, sauté the bacon on medium-low heat for 5 minutes, until browned and crisp. Remove the bacon and set it aside. Drain all the fat, except 2 tablespoons, from the pan. Add the garlic and cook for 30 seconds.

Deglaze the pan with the red wine and cook on high heat for 1 minute, scraping the bottom of the pan. Add the beef stock, tomato paste, thyme, 1 teaspoon salt, and $1/2$ teaspoon pepper. Bring to a boil and cook uncovered on medium-high heat for 10 minutes. Strain the sauce and return it to the pan. Add the onions and carrots and simmer uncovered for 20 to 30 minutes, until the sauce is reduced and the vegetables are cooked.

With a fork mash 2 tablespoons butter and the flour into a paste and whisk it gently into the sauce. Simmer for 2 minutes to thicken.

Meanwhile, sauté the mushrooms separately in 1 tablespoon butter and 1 tablespoon oil for about 10 minutes, until browned and tender.

Add the filet of beef slices, the mushrooms, and the bacon to the pan with the vegetables and sauce. Cover and reheat gently for 5 to 10 minutes. Do *not* overcook. Season to taste and serve immediately.

indonesian ginger chicken

SERVES 4 TO 6

This wonderful recipe comes from my friends Devon Fredericks and Susan Costner, who owned the legendary specialty food store Loaves and Fishes in the 1970s. They have extraordinary taste and style, and our variation of their recipe has been a Barefoot Contessa standard for many years. It is incredibly delicious, hot or cold, and is so easy to prepare. Lauren Bacall gets cranky if we are sold out.

1 CUP	*honey*
¾ CUP	*soy sauce*
¼ CUP	*minced garlic (8 to 12 cloves)*
½ CUP	*peeled and grated fresh ginger root*
2	*chickens (3½ pounds each), quartered, with backs removed*

Bell and Evans chickens are the best quality available commercially.

Cook the honey, soy sauce, garlic, and ginger root in a small saucepan over low heat until the honey is melted. Arrange the chicken in a large, shallow baking pan, skin side down, and pour on the sauce. Cover the pan tightly with aluminum foil. Marinate overnight in the refrigerator.

Preheat the oven to 350 degrees.

Place the baking pan in the oven and bake for ½ hour. Uncover the pan, turn the chicken skin side up, and raise the temperature to 375 degrees. Continue baking for 30 minutes, or until the juices run clear when you cut between the leg and the thigh and the sauce is a rich dark brown.

kitchen clambake

For years at Barefoot Contessa, we made this clambake at the beach. Not only did we have to dig a pit for cooking, but we had to deal with all that wind and sand and darkness. I finally got smart and decided to make a clambake in the kitchen. This is made in one huge pot and it's wonderful served with corn on the cob, a tomato salad, and lots of crusty French bread. And no sand.

1½ POUNDS	*kielbasa*
3 CUPS	*chopped yellow onions*
	(2 large onions)
2 CUPS	*chopped leeks, well cleaned*
	(2 leeks, white parts only)
¼ CUP	*good olive oil*
1½ POUNDS	*small potatoes (red or white)*
1 TABLESPOON	*kosher salt*
½ TABLESPOON	*ground black pepper*
2 DOZEN	*littleneck clams, scrubbed*
1 POUND	*steamer clams, scrubbed*
2 POUNDS	*mussels, cleaned and debearded*
1½ POUNDS	*large shrimp, in the shell*
3	*lobsters (1½ pounds each)*
2 CUPS	*good dry white wine*

I like to use white Châteauneuf du Pape or a good white Burgundy for the clambake and also to serve with dinner. It's an expensive ingredient, but it makes a wonderfully flavored broth.

Slice the kielbasa diagonally into 1-inch-thick slices. Set aside. Sauté the onions and leeks in the olive oil in a heavy-bottomed 16- to 20-quart stockpot on medium heat for 15 minutes, until the onions start to brown.

Layer the ingredients on top of the onions in the stockpot in this order: first the potatoes, salt, and pepper, then the kielbasa, littleneck clams, steamer clams, mussels, shrimp, and lobsters. Pour in the white wine. Cover the pot tightly and cook over medium-high heat until steam *just* begins to escape from the lid, about 15 minutes. Lower the heat to medium and cook another 15 minutes. The clambake should be done. Test to be sure the potatoes are tender, the lobsters are cooked, and the clams and mussels are open. Remove the lobsters to a wooden board, cut them up, and crack the claws. With large slotted spoons, remove the seafood, potatoes, and sausages to a large bowl and top with the lobsters. Season the broth in the pot to taste and serve immediately in mugs with the clambake.

lemon capellini
with caviar

SERVES 6

This is the perfect special appetizer or dinner for a celebration, such as New Year's Eve, but it needs to have the highest quality, freshest malossol caviar you can afford. It's dramatic, it's delicious, and best of all, it's ready in five minutes.

	Olive oil, for cooking the pasta
1 POUND	*dried capellini*
½ POUND	*unsalted butter, melted*
	Zest and juice of 2 lemons
1 TEASPOON	*kosher salt*
1 TEASPOON	*freshly ground white pepper*
150 GRAMS	*very good black caviar*
	Zest of 1 lemon, for garnish

Drizzle some olive oil in a large pot of boiling salted water, add the capellini, and cook al dente. Drain quickly, leaving a little water with the capellini. Quickly toss the capellini with the melted butter, lemon zest, lemon juice, salt, and pepper.

Place one serving of pasta on each plate and top with a large dollop of fresh caviar. Garnish with grated lemon zest. Serve immediately.

Sevruga caviar has the smallest grains and costs the least. Ossetra is larger and more expensive. Beluga is the largest and the most costly. I find ossetra the best quality for the money.

"Malossol" means "without salt" and indicates that the caviar is packed with a minimum of added salt.

perfect roast chicken

SERVES 3 TO 4

This is my husband's favorite Friday night dinner. It's a tradition with us. He has to drive 3¹/₂ hours to get home every weekend, and there's nothing like the smell of a fresh roast chicken to make him feel that the trip was worth it. Of course, I would never tell him that it is also the world's easiest dinner. I love to get the chickens at the Iaconos' farm in East Hampton. The chickens are plump and flavorful, the way I imagine they were before "fast" food was discovered.

1 5- TO 6-POUND	*roasting chicken*
	Kosher salt
	Freshly ground black pepper
1 LARGE BUNCH	*fresh thyme*
1	*lemon, halved*
1 HEAD	*garlic, cut in half crosswise*
2 TABLESPOONS	*butter, melted*
1	*Spanish onion, thickly sliced*
1 CUP	*chicken stock*
2 TABLESPOONS	*all-purpose flour*

Preheat the oven to 425 degrees.

Remove the chicken giblets. Rinse the chicken inside and out. Remove any excess fat and leftover pinfeathers and pat the outside dry. Place the chicken in a roasting pan. Liberally salt and pepper the inside of the chicken. Stuff the cavity with the bunch of thyme, both halves of the lemon, and all the garlic. Brush the outside of the chicken with the butter and sprinkle again with salt and pepper. Tie the legs together with kitchen string and tuck the wing tips under the body of the chicken. Scatter the onion slices around the chicken.

Roast the chicken for 1½ hours, or until the juices run clear when you cut between a leg and thigh. Remove to a platter and cover with aluminum foil while you prepare the gravy.

Remove all the fat from the bottom of the pan, reserving 2 tablespoons in a small cup. Add the chicken stock to the pan and cook on high heat for about 5 minutes, until reduced, scraping the bottom of the pan. Combine the 2 tablespoons of chicken fat with the flour and add to the pan. Boil for a few minutes to cook the flour. Strain the gravy into a small saucepan and season it to taste. Keep it warm over a very low flame while you carve the chicken.

Slice the chicken onto a platter and serve immediately with the warm gravy.

If you want to roast vegetables with the chicken, place 8 whole new red potatoes, 4 carrots, cut diagonally into quarters, and add them with the onions. Place the chicken on top of the vegetables for roasting.

lobster potpie

SERVES 4 TO 5

Who doesn't like homemade chicken potpie? A friend suggested we make lobster potpie and it sounded so good that I went directly home and made one. It keeps for months in the freezer. All you have to do is defrost one and pop it in the oven a few hours before guests arrive.

1½ CUPS	*chopped yellow onion (1 large onion)*
¾ CUP	*chopped fennel (1 fennel bulb)*
¼ POUND	*unsalted butter*
½ CUP	*all-purpose flour*
2½ CUPS	*fish stock or clam juice*
1 TABLESPOON	*Pernod*
1½ TEASPOONS	*kosher salt*
¾ TEASPOON	*freshly ground black pepper*
3 TABLESPOONS	*heavy cream*
¾ POUND	*cooked fresh lobster meat*
1½ CUPS	*frozen peas (not "baby" peas)*
1½ CUPS	*frozen small whole onions*
½ CUP	*minced flat-leaf parsley*

PASTRY

3 CUPS	*all-purpose flour*
1½ TEASPOONS	*salt*
1 TEASPOON	*baking powder*
8 TABLESPOONS	*cold fresh lard, diced (¼ pound)*
8 TABLESPOONS	*cold unsalted butter, diced*
½ TO ⅔ CUP	*ice water*
1	*egg, beaten with 1 tablespoon water or heavy cream, for egg wash*

Sauté the onions and fennel with the butter in a large sauté pan on medium heat until the onions are translucent, 10 to 15 minutes. Add the flour and cook on low heat for 3 more minutes, stirring occasionally. Slowly add the stock, Pernod, salt, and pepper and simmer for 5 more minutes. Add the heavy cream.

Cut the lobster meat into medium-sized cubes. Place the lobster, frozen peas, frozen onions, and parsley in a bowl (there is no need to defrost the vegetables). Pour the sauce over the mixture and check the seasonings. Set aside.

For the crust, mix the flour, salt, and baking powder in a food processor fitted with a metal blade. Add the lard and butter and pulse 10 times, until the fat is the size of peas. With the motor running, add the ice water; process only enough to moisten the dough and have it just come together. Dump the dough on a floured surface and knead quickly into a ball. Wrap the dough in plastic and allow it to rest for 30 minutes in the refrigerator.

Preheat the oven to 375 degrees.

Divide the dough in half and roll out each half to fit a 9- or 9½-inch-round by 2-inch-high ovenproof glass or ceramic baking dish. Place one crust in the dish, fill with the lobster mixture, and top with the second crust. Crimp the crusts together and brush with the egg wash. Make 4 or 5 slashes in the top crust and bake for 1 hour and 15 minutes, until the top is golden brown and the filling is bubbling hot.

You can also make shrimp or mixed seafood potpies; just substitute an equal amount of seafood for the lobster.

This can be prepared ahead of time, refrigerated, then baked before dinner.

Your fish market probably sells fresh fish stock.

salmon with fennel

SERVES 10 TO 15

I don't mind doing a little work to get a dinner party ready as long as I know there will be no last-minute crises. We have been making this salmon for years for parties and it comes out perfectly every time. Prepare the filling, tie the salmon, and either bake it right away or refrigerate it until 45 minutes before you want to serve it. In a preheated oven, a whole salmon will be perfectly cooked in exactly 30 minutes.

1 10-POUND	*fresh salmon*
5 CUPS	*sliced yellow onions, 1/4-inch thick (3 pounds)*
5 CUPS	*sliced fennel bulbs, 1/4-inch thick (3 pounds)*
1/2 CUP	*good olive oil*
3 TABLESPOONS	*fresh thyme leaves, coarsely chopped*
2 TABLESPOONS	*coarsely chopped fennel fronds*
	Zest of 1 orange
2 TABLESPOONS	*freshly squeezed orange juice*
2 TEASPOONS	*kosher salt*
1 TEASPOON	*freshly ground black pepper*

In a pinch, you can use two sides of salmon with the filling sandwiched in between.

Have the fishmonger cut the head and tail off the salmon and butterfly it, removing all the bones. You should have about 7 pounds of salmon.

Preheat the oven to 500 degrees.

Sauté the onions and fennel with the olive oil for 10 minutes on medium-high heat, stirring occasionally. Add the thyme leaves, fennel fronds, orange zest, orange juice, salt, and pepper and sauté for 5 more minutes, until the onions and fennel are tender. Taste for salt and pepper.

Lay the salmon, skin side down, on a cutting board and sprinkle both sides generously with salt and pepper. Spread the fennel filling over half of the salmon. Pull the other half up and over the filling, enclosing it. Tie the salmon every 2 inches with kitchen string to secure the stuffing.

Place a baking sheet lined with parchment paper in the oven for 5 minutes to heat it. Carefully transfer the salmon to the hot baking sheet and bake it for exactly 30 minutes (10 minutes for each inch of thickness). Do not overbake!

Allow to cool slightly, then remove the strings. To serve, cut into thick slices with a very sharp knife. This salmon is delicious hot or at room temperature.

A mandoline will make short work of all the slicing.

Onions are easier to slice if you leave the root intact after you cut them in half.

I like to use a hand zester, which makes strips of zest.

It's always a good idea to check your oven temperature with an oven thermometer.

I use kosher salt and cracked pepper to season the salmon fillets.

swordfish with tomatoes and capers

SERVES 4

This is a very simple dish that I make for summer parties. The sauce can be made well in advance and the fish grilled at the last minute. On a hot summer day, it's also delicious served cold. I have updated a Barefoot Contessa classic by adding fennel to give it more flavor. You can add any Provençal ingredients that you like: pitted niçoise olives, sautéed bell peppers, anchovies, even a garnish of steamed mussels.

1 CUP	*chopped yellow onion (1 onion)*
1 CUP	*chopped fennel (1 bulb)*
3 TABLESPOONS	*good olive oil*
1 TEASPOON	*minced garlic*
28 OUNCES	*canned plum tomatoes, drained*
1 TEASPOON	*kosher salt*
¾ TEASPOON	*freshly ground black pepper*
2 TABLESPOONS	*chicken stock*
2 TABLESPOONS	*good dry white wine*
½ CUP	*chopped fresh basil leaves*
2 TABLESPOONS	*capers, drained*
1 TABLESPOON	*unsalted butter*
4 1-INCH-THICK	*swordfish fillets (about 2½ pounds)*
	Fresh basil leaves

This sauce is also delicious with other grilled fish, such as cod or red snapper.

For the sauce, cook the onions and fennel in the oil in a large sauté pan on medium-low heat for 10 minutes, until the vegetables are soft. Add the garlic and cook for 30 seconds. Add the drained tomatoes, smashing them in the pan with a fork, plus the salt and pepper. Simmer on low heat for 15 minutes. Add the chicken stock and white wine and simmer for 10 more minutes to reduce the liquid. Add the basil, capers, and butter and cook for 1 minute more.

Prepare a grill with hot coals. Brush the swordfish with olive oil, and sprinkle with salt and pepper. Grill on high heat for 5 minutes on each side until the center is no longer raw. Do not overcook. Place the sauce on the bottom of a plate, arrange the swordfish on top, and garnish with basil leaves. Serve hot or at room temperature.

When it is too cold to grill outdoors, I use a cast-iron stove-top grill.

turkey meat loaf

SERVES 8 TO 10

This meat loaf is so loved at Barefoot Contessa that customers get very cranky if we run out. It tastes like old-fashioned meat loaf, but since it's made with ground turkey, it's also good for you. But then, of course, you have to serve it with Parmesan Smashed Potatoes (page 158). My husband loves when I make enough that he can have meat loaf sandwiches for days afterwards. This is a large recipe to ensure lots of leftovers.

This recipe can be halved to make a smaller meat loaf.

3 CUPS	*chopped yellow onions (2 large onions)*
2 TABLESPOONS	*good olive oil*
2 TEASPOONS	*kosher salt*
1 TEASPOON	*freshly ground black pepper*
1 TEASPOON	*fresh thyme leaves (1/2 teaspoon dried)*
1/3 CUP	*Worcestershire sauce*
3/4 CUP	*chicken stock*
1 1/2 TEASPOONS	*tomato paste*
5 POUNDS	*ground turkey breast*
1 1/2 CUPS	*plain dry bread crumbs*
3	*extra-large eggs, beaten*
3/4 CUP	*ketchup*

We like Heinz ketchup.

Preheat the oven to 325 degrees.

In a medium sauté pan, on medium-low heat, cook the onions, olive oil, salt, pepper, and thyme until the onions are translucent but not browned, approximately 15 minutes. Add the Worcestershire sauce, chicken stock, and tomato paste and mix well. Allow to cool to room temperature.

Combine the ground turkey, bread crumbs, eggs, and onion mixture in a large bowl. Mix well and shape into a rectangular loaf on an ungreased baking sheet. Spread the ketchup evenly on top. Bake for $1\frac{1}{2}$ hours, until the internal temperature is 160 degrees and the meat loaf is cooked through. (A pan of hot water in the oven, under the meat loaf, will keep the top from cracking.) Serve hot, room temperature, or cold in a sandwich.

grilled tuna niçoise platter

SERVES 8

This takes a bit of work in advance, but only needs "assembling" before guests arrive. Use your imagination to think of other Provençal ingredients you like and add them to the platter. The ingredients are simple, but the presentation makes it feel like a party.

8 1-INCH-THICK	*fresh tuna steaks (about 4 pounds)*
	Olive oil
	Kosher salt
	Freshly ground black pepper
¾ POUND	*haricots verts, stems removed*
	and blanched
1 RECIPE	*French Potato Salad (page 96)*
2 POUNDS	*ripe tomatoes, cut into wedges*
	(6 small tomatoes)
8	*hard-cooked eggs, peeled and cut in half*
½ POUND	*good black olives, pitted*
1 BUNCH	*watercress or arugula*
1 CAN	*anchovies (optional)*

VINAIGRETTE

3 TABLESPOONS	*champagne vinegar*
½ TEASPOON	*Dijon mustard*
½ TEASPOON	*kosher salt*
¼ TEASPOON	*freshly ground black pepper*
10 TABLESPOONS	*good olive oil*

To grill the tuna, get a charcoal or stove-top cast-iron grill very hot. Brush the fish with olive oil, and sprinkle with salt and pepper. Grill each side for only 1½ to 2 minutes. The center should be raw, like sushi, or the tuna will be tough and dry. Arrange the tuna, haricots verts, potato salad, tomatoes, eggs, olives, watercress, and anchovies, if used, on a large flat platter.

For the vinaigrette, combine the vinegar, mustard, salt, and pepper. Slowly whisk in the olive oil to make an emulsion. Drizzle some over the fish and vegetables and serve the rest in a pitcher on the side.

vegetables

Roasted Carrots

Roasted Brussels Sprouts

Caramelized Butternut Squash

Roasted Baby Pumpkins

Roasted Fennel with Parmesan

Homemade Applesauce

Potato-Fennel Gratin

Parmesan Smashed Potatoes

Fingerling Potatoes

Roasted Vegetable Torte

Spinach Pie

Vegetable Platter

eat your vegetables

When I was young I always hated vegetables. The object at dinner was feeding them to the dog (he'd eat anything) without Mom finding out. I think there were two things I hated about them. First, they were "good for me," which automatically made me suspicious. But most of all, they were odd flavors and textures.

Today, exactly what I hated about vegetables has become exactly what I love about them. First, they *are* good for me! But best of all, each vegetable has a distinct flavor and texture that I have come to appreciate. Fresh vegetables can be sweet like roasted butternut squash, spicy like grilled peppers, creamy like Parmesan smashed potatoes, and crisp like roasted Brussels sprouts. They can be made into layered tortes with eggplant and zucchini, baked in "pies" with spinach and feta cheese, or roasted in gratins with potatoes and fennel. We are all taught to dress with an interesting assortment of textures—a silk blouse with a wool skirt and chenille sweater, for example. I think of mixing vegetables with the same eye for color and texture.

The key to great vegetable cooking is great ingredients. In the spring, when the asparagus are young and sweet; in the summer, when the carrots are freshly dug; and in the autumn, when the fingerling potatoes are ready, I toss them with olive oil, coarse salt and fresh pepper, and roast them at a high temperature. It's so easy! It is important to remember that the better the ingredients, the less you need to do to make the dish taste good.

At Barefoot Contessa we make lots of vegetable platters for parties. I choose vegetables that have hot colors that seem to clash: carrots, beets, cherry tomatoes, purple onions, and yellow peppers. All together on one platter, there won't be any need for anyone to say, "Eat your vegetables."

roasted carrots

SERVES 6

Fresh carrots are sweet all year long, and this recipe has been a Barefoot Contessa standard. The key here is a very high oven temperature, which browns the carrots on the outside without drying them out on the inside. Of course, the sweeter the carrots, the better this will taste, so buy them from a farm whenever you can.

12 *carrots*
3 TABLESPOONS *good olive oil*
1¼ TEASPOONS *kosher salt*
½ TEASPOON *freshly ground black pepper*
2 TABLESPOONS *minced fresh dill or flat-leaf parsley*

Preheat the oven to 400 degrees.

If the carrots are thick, cut them in half lengthwise; if not, leave them whole. Slice the carrots diagonally into 1½-inch-thick slices. (The carrots will get smaller while cooking, so make the slices big.) Toss them in a bowl with the olive oil, salt, and pepper. Place on a baking sheet in one layer and roast in the oven for 20 minutes.

Toss the carrots with minced dill or parsley, season to taste, and serve.

At Barefoot Contessa, we skip the bowl and season the vegetables directly on the baking sheet.

roasted brussels sprouts

SERVES 6

All of us remember those boiled, mushy Brussels sprouts that your aunt served at Thanksgiving, but customers at Barefoot Contessa are surprised at how good this local winter vegetable can taste when it is roasted and crisp with lots of coarse salt.

1½ POUNDS *Brussels sprouts*

3 TABLESPOONS *good olive oil*

¾ TEASPOON *kosher salt*

½ TEASPOON *freshly ground black pepper*

Preheat the oven to 400 degrees.

Cut off the ends of the Brussels sprouts and pull off any yellow outer leaves. Mix them in a bowl with the olive oil, salt, and pepper. Turn them out on a baking sheet and roast for 35 to 40 minutes, until crisp outside and tender inside. Shake the pan from time to time, to brown the Brussels sprouts evenly. Sprinkle with more kosher salt (I like these salty like french fries) and serve.

Clean hands are a cook's best tools; use them for mixing the vegetables with oil.

caramelized butternut squash

SERVES 6 TO 8

We have so many orders for butternut squash around Thanksgiving that the cooks' hands turn yellow from peeling squash. For this recipe, I don't even bother using a bowl; I just mix the ingredients right on the baking sheet.

2	*medium butternut squash (4 to 5 pounds total)*
6 TABLESPOONS	*unsalted butter, melted*
¼ CUP	*light brown sugar, packed*
1½ TEASPOONS	*kosher salt*
½ TEASPOON	*freshly ground black pepper*

Preheat the oven to 400 degrees.

Cut off and discard the ends of each butternut squash. Peel the squash, cut them in half lengthwise, and remove the seeds. Cut the squash into 1¼- to 1½-inch cubes and place them on a baking sheet. Add the melted butter, brown sugar, salt, and pepper. With clean hands, toss all the ingredients together and spread in a single layer on the baking sheet. Roast for 45 to 55 minutes, until the squash is tender and the glaze begins to caramelize. While roasting, turn the squash a few times with a spatula, to be sure it browns evenly. Taste for seasonings and serve hot.

roasted baby pumpkins

SERVES 6

These little pumpkins are often used for decoration in autumn, but we love to bake them filled with homemade applesauce and serve them with roast chicken or turkey. They are delicious, and look festive on your plate.

6	*baby pumpkins*
	Kosher salt
	Freshly ground black pepper
1 CUP	*Homemade Applesauce (page 155)*
	or commercial

Choose pumpkins that are similar in size so they will all roast in the same time.

Preheat the oven to 350 degrees.

Cut off and reserve the tops of each pumpkin by cutting around the stem in a circle. Scoop out the seeds with a small spoon and liberally sprinkle the insides with salt and pepper. Place the pumpkins on a greased baking sheet and fill each one with applesauce. Place the tops back on and roast them for 45 minutes to 1 hour, or until the pumpkins are tender but not mushy.

roasted fennel
with parmesan

SERVES 6

Fennel has a distinctly licorice flavor when it is raw, but it is mild and sweet when it is cooked. I like to cook it so the edges are crisp and brown and the inside is tender. Aged Parmesan cheese adds the perfect kick.

4 *large fennel bulbs*

½ CUP *good olive oil*

1 TEASPOON *kosher salt*

½ TEASPOON *freshly ground black pepper*

2 TO 3 TABLESPOONS *freshly grated Parmesan cheese*

Always buy good, aged Parmesan cheese and always grate it yourself.

The fronds from the fennel stalks may be minced like dill and sprinkled on before serving.

Preheat the oven to 400 degrees.

Remove the stems of the fennel and slice the bulb in half lengthwise. With the cut side down, slice the bulb vertically into ½-inch-thick slices, cutting right through the core. Spread the fennel slices on a baking sheet, coat with olive oil, salt, and pepper and toss with your hands.

Roast the fennel slices for about an hour, turning them once after 30 minutes, until the edges are crisp and brown. Sprinkle with Parmesan cheese and roast for 5 more minutes. Taste for salt and pepper and serve.

homemade applesauce

MAKES 2½ QUARTS

This recipe comes from Brent Newsom, who is a wonderful friend and caterer in Bridgehampton. I love to make it when there is a chill in the air and the apples are crisp and flavorful. The more varieties you use, the more depth of flavor you'll have, so be creative. This recipe makes a lot, but it lasts for weeks; and you can serve it with breakfast on pancakes, with lunch for dessert, and for dinner with roast chicken or turkey.

	Zest and juice of 2 large navel oranges
	Zest and juice of 1 lemon
3 POUNDS	*Granny Smith apples (6 to 8 apples)*
3 POUNDS	*sweet red apples, such as Macoun, McIntosh, or Winesap (6 to 8 apples)*
½ CUP	*light brown sugar, packed*
¼ POUND	*unsalted butter*
2 TEASPOONS	*ground cinnamon*
½ TEASPOON	*ground allspice*

Preheat the oven to 350 degrees.

Place the zest and juice of the oranges and lemon in a large bowl. Peel, quarter, and core the apples and toss them in the juice. Pour the apples and juice into a nonreactive Dutch oven or enameled iron pot. Add the brown sugar, butter, cinnamon, and allspice and cover the pot. Bake for 1½ hours, or until all the apples are soft. Mix with a whisk until smooth. Serve warm or at room temperature.

I add the peels of 2 red apples during cooking, because they give the finished applesauce a nice rosy color. Fish out the peels after the apples are cooked.

You can use a grater or zester, but I find a hand zester very fast and I like the strips of zest in the applesauce.

Chinese cinnamon has the best flavor.

potato-fennel gratin

SERVES 10

I love to make potato gratin and fennel gratin, so I decided to combine the two. If you make this in an old French gratin dish, it looks wonderful and can go from the oven to the table with style. This gratin can be cooked days ahead and reheated at 350 degrees for about 30 minutes.

2	*small fennel bulbs*
1	*yellow onion, thinly sliced*
2 TABLESPOONS	*good olive oil*
1 TABLESPOON	*unsalted butter*
2	*pounds russet potatoes (4 large potatoes)*
2 CUPS	*plus 2 tablespoons heavy cream*
2½ CUPS	*grated Gruyère cheese (½ pound)*
1 TEASPOON	*kosher salt*
½ TEASPOON	*freshly ground black pepper*

Preheat the oven to 350 degrees.

Butter the inside of a 10 × 15 × 2-inch (10 cup) baking dish.

Remove the stalks from the fennel and cut the bulbs in half lengthwise. Remove the cores and thinly slice the bulbs crosswise, making approximately 4 cups of sliced fennel. Sauté the fennel and onions in the olive oil and butter on medium-low heat for 15 minutes, until tender.

Peel the potatoes, then thinly slice them by hand or with a mandoline. Mix the sliced potatoes in a large bowl with 2 cups of cream, 2 cups of Gruyère, salt, and pepper. Add the sautéed fennel and onion and mix well.

Pour the potatoes into the baking dish. Press down to smooth the potatoes. Combine the remaining 2 tablespoons of cream and ¹⁄₂ cup of Gruyère and sprinkle on the top. Bake for 1¹⁄₂ hours, until the potatoes are very tender and the top is browned and bubbly. Allow to set for 10 minutes and serve.

parmesan smashed potatoes

SERVES 6 TO 8

My friend Antonia Bellanca taught me this old family recipe: old-fashioned mashed potatoes with an Italian twist. Use an electric mixer and don't peel the potatoes.

3 POUNDS	*red potatoes, unpeeled*
1 TABLESPOON	*plus 2 teaspoons kosher salt*
1½ CUPS	*half-and-half*
¼ POUND	*unsalted butter*
½ CUP	*sour cream*
½ CUP	*freshly grated Parmesan cheese*
½ TEASPOON	*freshly ground black pepper*

Place the potatoes and 1 tablespoon of salt in a 4-quart saucepan with cold water to cover. Bring to a boil, lower the heat, and simmer covered for 25 to 35 minutes, until the potatoes are completely tender. Drain.

In a small saucepan, heat the half-and-half and butter.

Put the potatoes into the bowl of an electric mixer fitted with a paddle attachment and mix them for a few seconds on low speed, to break them up. Slowly add the hot cream and butter to the potatoes, mixing on the lowest speed (the last quarter of the cream and butter should be folded in by hand). Fold in the sour cream, Parmesan cheese, the remaining salt, and pepper; taste for seasoning and serve immediately. If the potatoes are too thick, add more hot cream and butter.

To reheat, place the smashed potatoes in an ovenproof baking dish and sprinkle with 2 tablespoons of Parmesan cheese. Bake at 400 degrees for 20 to 30 minutes, or until the top is browned and the potatoes are heated through.

fingerling potatoes

SERVES 6

In the autumn, when the farmers dig their potatoes, Jim Pike sells little fingerlings. They are small, sweet, and have a creamy texture. I think very little should be done with them so you can taste the earthiness of the potato itself. When the preparation is this simple, it is important to use the best ingredients; be sure to use a very good, fruity extra-virgin olive oil.

2½ POUNDS *fingerling potatoes, unpeeled*

1 TABLESPOON *plus 1 teaspoon kosher salt*

½ TEASPOON *freshly ground black pepper*

3 TABLESPOONS *extra-virgin olive oil*

I like Williams-Sonoma extra-virgin California olive oil (page 249).

Rinse the potatoes and put them in a large saucepan. Cover them with cold water, add 1 tablespoon of salt, and bring to a boil. Simmer uncovered for 15 to 20 minutes, until they are just tender.

Drain the potatoes in a colander and place a kitchen towel on top, allowing them to steam for 5 to 10 minutes. As soon as they are cool enough to handle, cut each potato in half lengthwise. Place the potatoes in a bowl with 1 teaspoon salt and the pepper. Drizzle with the olive oil. Toss well and serve immediately.

roasted vegetable torte

SERVES 6

*Paul Hodges invented this recipe at Barefoot Contessa, and it was an
immediate hit. Make it ahead of time and then cut it into wedges, like
a cake. The layers of roasted vegetables look so beautiful.*

2	*zucchini, cut into $^1/_4$-inch slices*
1	*red onion, cut in half lengthwise and sliced*
1 TEASPOON	*minced garlic*
	Good olive oil
	Kosher salt
	Freshly ground black pepper
2	*red bell peppers, halved, cored, and seeded*
2	*yellow bell peppers, halved, cored, and seeded*
1	*eggplant, unpeeled, cut into $^1/_4$-inch slices* *(1$^1/_2$ pounds)*
$^1/_2$ CUP	*freshly grated Parmesan cheese*

Preheat the oven to 400 degrees.

Cook the zucchini, onions, garlic, and 2 tablespoons olive oil
in a large sauté pan over medium heat for 10 minutes until the
zucchini is tender. Season with salt and pepper. Brush the red
and yellow peppers and eggplant with olive oil, season with salt
and pepper, and roast on a baking sheet for 30 to 40 minutes,
until soft but not browned.

In a 6-inch round cake pan, place each vegetable in a single,
overlapping layer, sprinkling Parmesan cheese and salt and pepper to taste between each of the layers of vegetables. Begin with
half of the eggplant, then layer half of the zucchini and onions,

then all of the red peppers, then all of the yellow peppers, then the rest of the zucchini and onions, and finally the rest of the eggplant. Cover the top of the vegetables with a 6-inch round of parchment paper or waxed paper. Place a 6-inch flat disk (another cake pan or the bottom of a false-bottom tart pan) on top and weight it with a heavy jar. Place on a plate or baking sheet (it will leak) and chill completely. Drain the liquids, place on a platter, and serve at room temperature.

spinach pie

SERVES 6 TO 8

This recipe is from my dear friend Brent Newsom of Brent Newsom Catering in Bridgehampton. When he is not taking care of customers, he is taking care of everyone else. This is like Greek spanakopita but with a lot more of that great filling. If you want to make this ahead of time, keep it wrapped in the refrigerator, and then serve it at room temperature or reheated.

3 CUPS	*chopped yellow onions (2 onions)*
2 TABLESPOONS	*good olive oil*
2 TEASPOONS	*kosher salt*
1½ TEASPOONS	*freshly ground black pepper*
3 (10-OUNCE)	*packages frozen chopped spinach, defrosted*
6	*extra-large eggs, beaten*
2 TEASPOONS	*grated nutmeg*
½ CUP	*freshly grated Parmesan cheese*
3 TABLESPOONS	*plain dry bread crumbs*
½ POUND	*good feta, cut into ½-inch cubes*
½ CUP	*pignoli (pine nuts)*
¼ POUND	*salted butter, melted*
6 SHEETS	*phyllo dough, defrosted*

Preheat the oven to 375 degrees.

In a medium sauté pan on medium heat, sauté the onions with the olive oil until translucent and slightly browned, 10 to 15 minutes. Add the salt and pepper and allow to cool slightly.

Squeeze out and discard as much of the liquid from the spinach as possible. Put the spinach into a bowl and then gently mix in the onions, eggs, nutmeg, Parmesan cheese, bread crumbs, feta, and pignoli.

Butter an ovenproof, nonstick, 8-inch sauté pan and line it with 6 stacked sheets of phyllo dough, brushing each with melted butter and letting the edges hang over the pan. Pour the spinach mixture into the middle of the phyllo and neatly fold the edges up and over the top to seal in the filling. Brush the top well with melted butter. Bake for 1 hour, until the top is golden brown and the filling is set. Remove from the oven and allow to cool completely. Serve at room temperature.

vegetable platter

Vegetable platters are so very easy to do at home; you can cook all the vegetables yourself or add some prepared vegetables that you buy from a specialty food store. I like to combine the flavors of grilled vegetables, roasted vegetables, and even boiled potatoes and beets. Be inventive, but mix the colors and textures to make a beautiful arrangement. I allow a half pound of vegetables per person.

grilled vegetables

Toss each vegetable with olive oil, kosher salt, and freshly ground black pepper. Grill over hot coals or on a cast-iron stove-top grill until soft and charred, approximately 15 to 20 minutes.

Bell peppers, seeded and cut into quarters
Zucchini, sliced diagonally 1/2 inch thick
Eggplant, unpeeled, sliced crosswise 1/2 inch thick
Red onions, sliced 1/2 inch thick
Asparagus, tough ends removed
Beets, unpeeled, sliced 1/2 inch thick

roasted vegetables

Toss each vegetable with olive oil, kosher salt, and freshly ground black pepper. Roast in a preheated 400-degree oven for 20 to 40 minutes, until tender on the inside and crisp on the outside.

Carrots (recipe, page 149)
Brussels sprouts (recipe, page 150)
Fennel (recipe, page 154)
Butternut squash (recipe, page 151)
New potatoes, unpeeled, cut into quarters
Sweet potatoes, unpeeled, sliced 1/2 inch thick
Beets, unpeeled, cut into quarters

Arrange the vegetables in groups on a large platter. Sprinkle with salt and pepper. Serve either hot or at room temperature. I like to arrange the vegetables on an ovenproof ironstone platter and put it in a 150-degree oven to stay warm until dinner is served.

desserts

Outrageous Brownies

Coconut Cupcakes

Shortbread Hearts

"Linzer" Cookies

Pecan Shortbread

Raspberry Tart

Fresh Fruit Tart

Lime Curd Tart

Pecan Squares

Peach and Raspberry Crisp

Croissant Bread Pudding

Chocolate Buttercream Cake

Pastry Cream

Honey Vanilla Crème Fraîche

Vanilla Extract

Country Dessert Platter

desserts to remember

Who doesn't love goodies from a bakery? Just take a small child past a display of cookies in the window and you know how basic that desire is. Even better is dessert from your own kitchen, with the smells of sugar and spice in the mixing bowl, and the aroma of warm peach and raspberry crisp from the oven. I'm sure my husband's affection for me was initially linked to the boxes of homemade brownies I used to send to him in college.

Dessert has a lot to do with how people feel about a dinner. The main course can be as simple as a hearty soup and a tossed salad, but what we really remember is the rich lime tart or the sinful pecan bars that came at the end. My experience in the store is that people are very conscious about eating lighter meals, but they never skip dessert, even if it's just a shortbread cookie and clementines.

Baking is a very different skill from cooking. Cooking is more casual—you can throw in new ingredients while you're working and tasting. Baking, on the other hand, generally requires exact measurements of flour, sugar, butter, and eggs, plus details like sifting the flour and having the butter at room temperature. The more you get into the habit of using ingredients properly, the better your baking will be. The simple part is that almost all cake recipes have the same basic formula: cream room-temperature butter with sugar; then add room-temperature eggs; then add dry ingredients (flour, leavening, salt, etc.) alternately with wet ingredients (milk, vanilla, flavorings, etc.). If you follow these steps carefully, you will bake successfully every time.

As children, we were taught that dessert was the reward at the end of the meal. A homemade dessert is a special reward. I hope you'll enjoy baking and serving these desserts as much as I do.

outrageous brownies

MAKES 20 LARGE BROWNIES

Inspiration for this recipe came from the Chocolate Glob in the SoHo Charcuterie Cookbook *published by William Morrow in 1983. In its heyday, the SoHo Charcuterie was the cutting edge of New York restaurants. The giant confection was a blob of chocolate dough filled with chocolate chips and nuts. I thought I could make a brownie with almost the same formula. They've been flying out the door for fifteen years!*

1 POUND	*unsalted butter*
1 POUND	*plus 12 ounces semisweet chocolate chips*
6	*ounces unsweetened chocolate*
6	*extra-large eggs*
3 TABLESPOONS	*instant coffee granules*
2 TABLESPOONS	*pure vanilla extract*
2¼ CUPS	*sugar*
1¼ CUPS	*all-purpose flour*
1 TABLESPOON	*baking powder*
1 TEASPOON	*salt*
3 CUPS	*chopped walnuts*

We find that Hershey's chocolate chips work very well.

Preheat the oven to 350 degrees.

Butter and flour a 12 × 18 × 1-inch baking sheet.

Melt together the butter, 1 pound of chocolate chips, and the unsweetened chocolate in a medium bowl over simmering water. Allow to cool slightly. In a large bowl, stir (do not beat) together the eggs, coffee granules, vanilla, and sugar. Stir the warm chocolate mixture into the egg mixture and allow to cool to room temperature.

In a medium bowl, sift together 1 cup of flour, the baking powder, and salt. Add to the cooled chocolate mixture. Toss the walnuts and 12 ounces of chocolate chips in a medium bowl with ¼ cup of flour, then add them to the chocolate batter. Pour into the baking sheet.

Bake for 20 minutes, then rap the baking sheet against the oven shelf to force the air to escape from between the pan and the brownie dough. Bake for about 15 minutes, until a toothpick comes out clean. Do not overbake! Allow to cool thoroughly, refrigerate, and cut into 20 large squares.

Flouring the chips and walnuts keeps them from sinking to the bottom.

It is very important to allow the batter to cool well before adding the chocolate chips, or the chips will melt and ruin the brownies.

This recipe can be baked up to a week in advance, wrapped in plastic, and refrigerated.

coconut cupcakes

When someone stops me on the street and says, "You know what I love in your store?" I know the answer is probably going to be these cupcakes. People are devoted to them. I'm not sure if it's the cupcake or the icing, but the combination is positively heavenly.

¾ POUND	*unsalted butter at room temperature*
2 CUPS	*sugar*
5	*extra-large eggs at room temperature*
1½ TEASPOONS	*pure vanilla extract*
1½ TEASPOONS	*pure almond extract*
3 CUPS	*all-purpose flour*
1 TEASPOON	*baking powder*
½ TEASPOON	*baking soda*
½ TEASPOON	*salt*
1 CUP	*buttermilk*
14 OUNCES	*sweetened, shredded coconut*
	Cream Cheese Icing (recipe follows)

Preheat the oven to 325 degrees.

In the bowl of an electric mixer fitted with a paddle attachment, cream the butter and sugar until light and fluffy, about 5 minutes. With the mixer running on low, add the eggs one at a time, scraping down the bowl after each addition. Add the vanilla and almond extracts and mix well.

In a separate bowl, sift together the flour, baking powder, baking soda, and salt. In three parts, alternately add the dry

continued next page

ingredients and the buttermilk to the batter, beginning and ending with the dry. Mix until *just* combined. Fold in 7 ounces of coconut.

I use an ice cream scoop to fill the muffin cups.

Line a muffin pan with paper liners. Fill each cup to the top with batter. Bake for 25 to 35 minutes, until the tops are brown and a toothpick comes out clean. Allow to cool in the pan for 15 minutes. Remove to a baking rack and cool completely. Frost with cream cheese icing and sprinkle with the remaining coconut.

cream cheese icing

FOR 18 TO 20 LARGE CUPCAKES

1 POUND	*cream cheese at room temperature*
¾ POUND	*unsalted butter at room temperature*
1 TEASPOON	*pure vanilla extract*
½ TEASPOON	*pure almond extract*
1½ POUNDS	*confectioners' sugar, sifted*

It is very important that the cream cheese and butter are at room temperature and that the confectioners' sugar is sifted to ensure no lumps in the icing.

In the bowl of an electric mixer fitted with a paddle attachment, blend together the cream cheese, butter, and vanilla and almond extracts. Add the confectioners' sugar and mix until smooth.

shortbread hearts

MAKES 24 HEARTS

These shortbread cookies come from the brilliant Eli Zabar of E.A.T., the Vinegar Factory, and Across the Street in New York City. They are the quintessence of shortbread and have been my all-time favorite cookie since the first time I tried one, over fifteen years ago. We also use the dough for lots of variations on this recipe — "Linzer" Cookies (page 178), Pecan Shortbread (page 181), and even Raspberry Tart (page 182).

¾ POUND	*unsalted butter at room temperature*
1 CUP	*sugar (plus extra for sprinkling)*
1 TEASPOON	*pure vanilla extract*
3½ CUPS	*all-purpose flour*
¼ TEASPOON	*salt*

Preheat the oven to 350 degrees.

In the bowl of an electric mixer fitted with a paddle attachment, mix together the butter and 1 cup of sugar until they are just combined. Add the vanilla. In a medium bowl, sift together the flour and salt, then add them to the butter-and-sugar mixture. Mix on low speed until the dough starts to come together. Dump onto a surface dusted with flour and shape into a flat disk. Wrap in plastic and chill for 30 minutes.

Roll the dough ½-inch thick and cut with a 3-inch heart-shaped cutter. Place the hearts on an ungreased baking sheet and sprinkle with sugar. Bake for 20 to 25 minutes, until the edges begin to brown.

Allow to cool to room temperature.

I find the edges of shortbread are ever so slightly sharper if you chill the cookies for ten minutes before you bake them.

Shortbread can be cut into shapes and refrigerated for a week and then baked the day you serve them.

"linzer" cookies

MAKES 14 TO 16 COOKIES

This is a variation of Eli Zabar's delicious shortbread cookies. It's not a traditional linzer because it isn't made with ground nuts, but I love the combination of shortbread and raspberries. The cookies can be made days in advance, wrapped with plastic, and assembled before serving.

¾ POUND *unsalted butter at room temperature*

1 CUP *granulated sugar*

1 TEASPOON *pure vanilla extract*

3½ CUPS *all-purpose flour*

¼ TEASPOON *salt*

¾ CUP *good raspberry preserves*
Confectioners' sugar, for dusting

Preheat the oven to 350 degrees.

In the bowl of an electric mixer fitted with the paddle attachment, mix together the butter and sugar until they are just combined. Add the vanilla. In a medium bowl, sift together the flour and salt, then add them to the butter-and-sugar mixture. Mix on low speed until the dough starts to come together. Dump onto a surface dusted with flour and shape into a flat disk. Wrap in plastic and chill for 30 minutes.

Roll the dough ¼-inch thick and cut 2¾-inch rounds with a plain or fluted cutter. With half of the rounds, cut a circle out of the middle with a 1-inch cutter. Place all the cookies on an ungreased baking sheet and chill for 15 minutes.

Bake the cookies for 20 to 25 minutes, until the edges begin to brown. Allow to cool to room temperature. Spread raspberry preserves on the flat side of each solid cookie. Dust the top of the cut-out cookies with confectioners' sugar and press the flat sides together, with the raspberry preserves in the middle and the confectioners' sugar on the top.

pecan shortbread

This is another variation we invented for Eli Zabar's wonderful short-bread cookie. You can use any nuts and flavorings you like, to give these a different taste.

¾ POUND	*unsalted butter at room temperature*
1 CUP	*sugar*
1 TEASPOON	*pure vanilla extract*
1 TEASPOON	*pure almond extract*
3½ CUPS	*all-purpose flour*
¼ TEASPOON	*salt*
1½ CUPS	*small-diced pecans*

Preheat the oven to 350 degrees.

In the bowl of an electric mixer fitted with a paddle attachment, mix together the butter and sugar until they are just combined. Add the vanilla and almond extracts. In a medium bowl, sift together the flour and salt, then add them to the butter-and-sugar mixture. Add the pecans and mix on low speed until the dough starts to come together. Dump onto a surface dusted with flour and shape into a flat disk. Wrap in plastic and chill for 30 minutes.

Roll the dough ½-inch thick and cut into 2½-inch squares with a plain or fluted cutter (or cut into any shape you like). Place the cookies on an ungreased baking sheet.

Bake for 20 to 25 minutes, until the edges begin to brown. Allow to cool to room temperature and serve.

To give pecans extra flavor, roast them on a baking sheet at 350 degrees for 8 minutes before dicing.

raspberry tart

MAKES ONE 9-INCH-SQUARE OR 10-INCH-ROUND TART;
SERVES 10 TO 12

For this shortbread crust, you just press the dough into the pan rather than rolling it out. I love the combination of shortbread and raspberries and so do our customers. For fun, bake the tart shell in advance and have one of your guests arrange the raspberries on top while you finish preparing dinner.

TART SHELL

¾ CUP	*unsalted butter at room temperature*
½ CUP	*sugar*
½ TEASPOON	*pure vanilla extract*
1¾ CUPS	*all-purpose flour*
PINCH	*salt*

FILLING

1 CUP	*good raspberry preserves*
1½ PINTS	*fresh raspberries (3 packages)*

Preheat the oven to 350 degrees.

In the bowl of an electric mixer fitted with a paddle attachment, mix the butter and sugar together until they are just combined. Add the vanilla. In a medium bowl, sift together the flour and salt, then add them to the butter-and-sugar mixture. Mix on low speed until the dough starts to come together. Dump onto a surface dusted with flour and shape into a flat disk. Press the dough into a 10-inch-round or 9-inch-square false-bottom tart pan, making sure that the finished edge is flat. Chill until firm.

Butter one side of a square of aluminum foil to fit inside the tart and place it, buttered side down, on the pastry. Fill with beans or rice. Bake for 20 minutes. Remove the foil and beans, prick the tart all over with the tines of a fork, and bake again for 20 to 25 minutes more, or until lightly browned. Allow to cool to room temperature.

Spread the tart with raspberry preserves and place the raspberries, stem end down, in concentric circles. If you are making a square tart, place the raspberries in rows. Serve immediately.

The tart shell can be baked a day ahead, and the tart can be assembled a few hours before serving. Never refrigerate a baked shell or a finished tart.

White raspberries are a special treat when they're in season.

fresh fruit tart

MAKES ONE 10-INCH-ROUND TART; SERVES 10 TO 12

In Paris, bakers make fresh fruit tarts that look like market baskets of fruit, sort of the way we make crudités here, but with fruit. It looks casual and gorgeous and encourages you to use whatever perfect fruit is in season.

To make individual tarts, press the dough into five 4¹/₂-inch tart pans and bake. Fill with raspberry preserves or pastry cream and fresh fruit.

1 10-INCH *baked tart shell (page 182)*

Raspberry preserves or

pastry cream (page 197)

SELECT FRUIT FROM THE FOLLOWING LIST:

Raspberries

Blueberries

Strawberries, cut in half, stems attached

Grapes, in small clusters

Peaches, peeled and sliced

Pears, sliced

Kiwi, peeled and sliced

Mangoes, peeled and sliced

Papayas, peeled and sliced

Fresh figs, halved or quartered

Fresh apricots, halved

Bananas, peeled and sliced

Plums, halved or quartered

Limes, very thinly sliced

Lemons, very thinly sliced

Follow the method for the raspberry tart (page 182).

After adding the preserves or pastry cream to the tart shell, group each fruit to make a casual arrangement, as in the photograph. Place the larger fruit first and then spill the berries into the spaces to fill in. Use one strong color, such as halved strawberries or a small bunch of red grapes, near the middle to give the design focus and height.

lime curd tart

I like lime curd with character. Lime curd is wonderful on a slice of toast, for dipping long-stemmed strawberries in, or to serve with pound cake and fresh fruit. Here we use it to fill a prebaked tart shell. Grating the zest in the food processor is very quick. Lime curd lasts for weeks in the refrigerator.

4	*limes at room temperature*
1½ CUPS	*sugar*
¼ POUND	*unsalted butter at room temperature*
4	*extra-large eggs at room temperature*
⅛ TEASPOON	*salt*
1 10-INCH	*baked tart shell (page 182) or*
	5 4½-inch baked tart shells

For lemon or orange curd, substitute equal measures of lemon or orange for the lime in this recipe.

Remove the zest of 4 limes with a vegetable peeler or zester, being careful to avoid the white pith. Squeeze the limes to make ½ cup of juice and set the juice aside. Put the zest in a food processor fitted with a steel blade. Add the sugar and process for 2 to 3 minutes, until the zest is very finely minced. In the bowl of an electric mixer fitted with a paddle attachment, cream the butter with the sugar and lime zest. Add the eggs, one at a time, and then add the lime juice and salt. Mix until combined.

Pour the mixture into a 2-quart saucepan and cook over low heat, stirring constantly, until thickened, about 10 minutes. The lime curd will thicken at about 175 degrees, or just below a simmer. Remove from the heat and set aside.

Fill the tart shell(s) with warm lime curd and allow to set at room temperature.

pecan squares

MAKES 20 LARGE SQUARES

This is like pecan pie with a shortbread crust. We make it all year long, and when we want to go "over the top," we dip half of each square in warm chocolate.

The filling will bubble over the edge. Place a larger baking sheet or aluminum foil on a lower oven rack, to catch the drips.

Make these bars with different kinds of nuts to vary the flavor. I like a mixture of pecans, peanuts, and walnuts.

Wrapped well and refrigerated, these bars will last for a week.

CRUST

1¼ POUNDS	*unsalted butter at room temperature*
¾ CUP	*granulated sugar*
3	*extra-large eggs*
¾ TEASPOON	*pure vanilla extract*
4½ CUPS	*all-purpose flour*
½ TEASPOON	*baking powder*
¼ TEASPOON	*salt*

TOPPING

1 POUND	*unsalted butter*
1 CUP	*good honey*
3 CUPS	*light brown sugar, packed*
1 TEASPOON	*grated lemon zest*
1 TEASPOON	*grated orange zest*
¼ CUP	*heavy cream*
2 POUNDS	*pecans, coarsely chopped*

Preheat the oven to 350 degrees.

For the crust, beat the butter and granulated sugar in the bowl of an electric mixer fitted with a paddle attachment, until light, approximately 3 minutes. Add the eggs and the vanilla and mix well. Sift together the flour, baking powder, and salt. Mix the dry ingredients into the batter with the mixer on low speed until just combined. Press the dough evenly into an ungreased 18 × 12 × 1-inch baking sheet, making an edge around the outside. It will be very sticky; sprinkle the dough and your hands lightly with flour. Bake for 15 minutes, until the crust is set but not browned. Allow to cool.

For the topping, combine the butter, honey, brown sugar, and zests in a large, heavy-bottomed saucepan. Cook over low heat until the butter is melted, using a wooden spoon to stir. Raise the heat and boil for 3 minutes. Remove from the heat. Stir in the heavy cream and pecans. Pour over the crust, trying not to get the filling between the crust and the pan. Bake for 25 to 30 minutes, until the filling is set. Remove from the oven and allow to cool. Wrap in plastic wrap and refrigerate until cold. Cut into bars and serve.

peach and raspberry crisp

SERVES 10

I love to make crisps all year long, but I pick whatever fruit is in season for the best flavor. During the summer, local yellow and white peaches are sweet and juicy and make delicious crisps. Serve this warm from the oven, with rum-flavored whipped cream or vanilla ice cream.

4 to 5 POUNDS	*firm, ripe peaches (10 to 12 large peaches)*
	Zest of 1 orange
1¼ CUPS	*granulated sugar*
1 CUP	*light brown sugar, packed*
1½ CUPS	*plus 2 to 3 tablespoons all-purpose flour*
½ PINT	*raspberries*
¼ TEASPOON	*salt*
1 CUP	*quick-cooking oatmeal*
½ POUND	*cold unsalted butter, diced*

Preheat the oven to 350 degrees. Butter the inside of a 10 × 15 × 2½-inch oval baking dish.

Immerse the peaches in boiling water for 30 seconds, then place them in cold water. Peel the peaches and slice them into thick wedges and place them into a large bowl. Add the orange zest, ¼ cup granulated sugar, ½ cup brown sugar, and 2 tablespoons of flour. Toss well. Gently mix in the raspberries. Allow the mixture to sit for 5 minutes. If there is a lot of liquid, add 1 more tablespoon of flour. Pour the peaches into the baking dish and gently smooth the top.

Combine 1½ cups flour, 1 cup granulated sugar, ½ cup

brown sugar, salt, oatmeal, and the cold, diced butter in the bowl of an electric mixer fitted with a paddle attachment. Mix on low speed until the butter is pea-sized and the mixture is crumbly. Sprinkle evenly on top of the peaches and raspberries. Bake for 1 hour, until the top is browned and crisp and the juices are bubbly. Serve immediately, or store in the refrigerator and reheat in a 350 degree oven for 20 to 30 minutes, until warm.

croissant bread pudding

SERVES 8 TO 10

I love to take a familiar flavor and then push it over the top! Everyone knows bread pudding with boring white bread, but this recipe uses light and flaky croissants, which add wonderful texture and richness, and lots of pure vanilla. I serve this with rum-flavored whipped cream, and guests always come back for seconds.

3	*extra-large whole eggs*
8	*extra-large egg yolks*
5 CUPS	*half-and-half*
1½ CUPS	*sugar*
1½ TEASPOONS	*pure vanilla extract*
6	*croissants, preferably stale*
1 CUP	*raisins*

Preheat the oven to 350 degrees.

In a medium bowl, whisk together the whole eggs, yolks, half-and-half, sugar, and vanilla. Set the custard mixture aside. Slice the croissants in half, horizontally. In a $10 \times 15 \times 2\frac{1}{2}$-inch oval baking dish, distribute the bottoms of the sliced croissants, then add the raisins, then the tops of the croissants (brown side up), being sure the raisins are between the layers of croissants or they will burn while baking. Pour the custard over the croissants and allow to soak for 10 minutes, pressing down gently.

Place the pan in a larger one filled with an inch of hot water. Cover the larger pan with aluminum foil, tenting the foil so it doesn't touch the pudding. Cut a few holes in the foil to allow steam to escape. Bake for 45 minutes. Uncover and bake for 40 to 45 more minutes or until the pudding puffs up and the custard is set. Remove from the oven and cool slightly.

This can also be made with brioche or other egg breads.

chocolate buttercream cake

SERVES 8 TO 10

This traditional chocolate layer cake comes from Larry Hayden, former pastry chef at Union Square Café and cookbook writer. We have been lucky to have him with us at Barefoot Contessa and he has taught us many wonderful recipes, including the whipped cream cake he is finishing in the photograph (above).

1¾ CUPS	*all-purpose flour*
1 CUP	*good cocoa powder*
1½ TEASPOONS	*baking soda*
¼ TEASPOON	*salt*
¾ CUP	*unsalted butter at room temperature*
⅔ CUP	*granulated sugar*
⅔ CUP	*light brown sugar, packed*
2	*extra-large eggs at room temperature*
2 TEASPOONS	*pure vanilla extract*
1 CUP	*buttermilk at room temperature*
½ CUP	*sour cream at room temperature*
2 TABLESPOONS	*brewed coffee*
	Chocolate Buttercream (recipe follows)

Callebaut and Valrhôna make excellent cocoa powders.

To avoid getting egg shells in the batter, always crack eggs on the counter rather than on the edge of the bowl.

Preheat the oven to 350 degrees. Butter two 8-inch round cake pans. Line the bottoms with wax paper, butter the paper, and dust the pans with flour, knocking out any excess. In a medium bowl, sift together the flour, cocoa, baking soda, and salt.

In the bowl of an electric mixer fitted with a paddle attachment, cream the butter and sugars on high speed until light, approximately 5 minutes. Add the eggs and vanilla and mix well. Combine the buttermilk, sour cream, and coffee. On low speed, add the flour mixture and the buttermilk mixture alternately in thirds, beginning with the buttermilk mixture and ending with the flour mixture. Mix the batter only until blended.

Divide the batter between the two pans and smooth the tops with a spatula. Bake on the middle rack of the oven for 25 to 30 minutes, or until a toothpick comes out clean. Cool for 10 minutes on a rack, remove from the pans, and allow to finish cooling.

continued next page

Place one cake on a serving plate, flat side up. Frost the top of that layer with buttercream. Place the second layer on top, also flat side up, and frost the top and sides.

chocolate buttercream

10 OUNCES	*bittersweet chocolate*
8 OUNCES	*semisweet chocolate*
½ CUP	*egg whites (3 extra-large eggs)*
	at room temperature
1 CUP	*granulated sugar*
PINCH	*cream of tartar*
½ TEASPOON	*salt*
1 POUND	*unsalted butter at room temperature*
2 TEASPOONS	*pure vanilla extract*
2 TEASPOONS	*instant espresso powder,*
	dissolved in 1 teaspoon water
2 TABLESPOONS	*dark rum, optional*

Chop the chocolates and melt in a bowl over simmering water until smooth. Allow to cool.

Mix the egg whites, sugar, cream of tartar, and salt in the bowl of an electric mixer fitted with a whisk. Heat the egg whites in the bowl over simmering water until they are warm to the touch, about 5 minutes. Whisk on high speed for 5 minutes, or until the meringue is cool and holds a stiff peak.

Add the butter, 1 tablespoon at a time, while beating on medium speed. Scrape down the bowl, add the chocolate, vanilla, espresso, and rum, if using, and mix for 1 minute or until the chocolate is completely blended in. If the buttercream seems very soft, allow it to cool, and beat it again.

pastry cream

6 *extra-large egg yolks*
at room temperature

¾ CUP *sugar*

3 TABLESPOONS *cornstarch*

2 CUPS *whole milk*

2 TABLESPOONS *unsalted butter*

1 TEASPOON *pure vanilla extract*

2 TABLESPOONS *heavy cream*

1 TEASPOON *Cognac or brandy*

In the bowl of an electric mixer fitted with a paddle attachment, beat the egg yolks and sugar on medium-high speed for about 3 minutes, until the mixture is light yellow and falls back into the bowl in a ribbon. On low speed, beat in the cornstarch. Bring the milk to a boil in a large saucepan and, with the mixer on low, slowly pour it into the egg mixture. Then pour the mixture back into the saucepan.

Cook over medium heat, stirring constantly with a whisk or wooden spoon, until the mixture is thick, about 10 minutes. Bring to a boil and cook on low heat 2 to 3 more minutes. Taste to be sure the cornstarch is cooked. Remove from the heat, mix in the butter, vanilla, cream, and Cognac and strain into a bowl. Place plastic wrap directly on the custard and refrigerate until cold.

honey vanilla crème fraîche

SERVES 6

I often say that from mistakes come the best surprises. Once, I was making a dessert that turned out horribly, and I had no time to redo it before my guests arrived. I tore the refrigerator apart, looking for a last-minute idea. Fortunately, I was able to invent this sauce. It is delicious served over fresh berries and peaches or on a slice of pound cake from a bakery.

Crème fraîche is a French clotted cream that is available in specialty food stores and is now also made in this country.

1 PINT	*crème fraîche*
3 TABLESPOONS	*good honey*
½ TEASPOON	*pure vanilla extract*
	Seeds scraped or squeezed
	from ½ vanilla bean

This can either be thin like a sauce or thick like whipped cream. For the sauce, simply combine all the ingredients with a spoon. To make it thick, place all the ingredients in the bowl of an electric mixer fitted with the whisk attachment and mix on high speed for about 60 seconds, or until it is as thick as whipped cream.

vanilla extract

Anna Pump from Loaves and Fishes in Sagaponack showed me how to make my own vanilla extract. Find a tall bottle that will hold at least a dozen vanilla beans. Fill the bottle with vodka. Let the beans marinate in the vodka for at least a month, and then you will have two wonderful ingredients for cooking and baking. First, the vodka will become vanilla extract, but more important, you can snip off one end of a vanilla bean and squeeze out all of the seeds for baking uses. This "brew" can continue for years by just adding more vanilla beans and more vodka. I've had mine stored on a shelf in the pantry for almost twenty years!

country dessert platter

This is an incredibly easy platter to arrange, even if you don't have time to bake! Buy a delicious and beautiful assortment of cookies, bars, and pastries from your local bakery and you're almost done. At Barefoot Contessa, I choose things that are both colorful and easy to eat with fingers. Remember, lots of baked goods look delicious on their own, but grouped together, they can look very brown. I mix colorful things like lemon bars, pecan bars, brownies, cookies, strawberries, figs, and slices of lemon cake.

Start with a platter that is round or oval and particularly one that is very flat. I like to use something simple, such as silver or china. Place doilies on the bottom of the platter. Cut each cake or bar into large bite-sized pieces; pastries cut too small tend to look like a dog's breakfast, too large and the platter looks unapproachable. I like to cut our large brownies into two finger-sized pieces and to cut the slices of cake in half.

The design of the platter is very simple. I follow good Japanese principles. "Earth" is a solid element, which grounds the design; "sky" is something taller, which curves upward; and "water" is something spilling forward. In all good design, the eye wants to be drawn to one focal point. I arrange slices of cake down the middle of the platter to give the arrangement grounding. I place the pastries in paper muffin cups and arrange them in a flowing pattern around the cake. Then I pile strawberries and figs or grapes high to give some height to the design. Then I add some cookies and lemon or hydrangea leaves to fill in the spaces.

I tend to prefer platters that appear more casual than formal. There's a fine balance, however, between casual and just plain messy. I think if you follow these simple steps, no matter which pastries or fruit you use, you will be thrilled with the results.

breakfast

The Perfect Cup of Coffee

Homemade Granola

Banana Crunch Muffins

Raspberry Corn Muffins

Cranberry Harvest Muffins

Cheddar-Dill Scones

Strawberry Scones

Maple-Oatmeal Scones

Hot Chocolate

White Hot Chocolate

Orange Yogurt

Fresh Fruit Platter

breakfast with friends

It's the beginning of the day, the sun has just come up, and the world is full of promise. And, of course, there is good coffee and great things to eat. I can start each day with a steaming bowl of hot oatmeal flavored with good maple syrup or with home-baked cranberry muffins, which I mixed the night before and pop into the oven while I stretch and yawn.

That said, I also love to invite friends for breakfast. Not really early, when I wake up, but later on Sunday, around 10 or 11 o'clock if I have no plans for lunch. The meal is really easy to make—more like arranging than cooking. For festive occasions, such as New Year's Day, I like to start with freshly squeezed blood-orange juice and champagne. But on most days, hot chocolate or French-roast coffee in a big café au lait cup is all anyone really wants. Breakfast can be baskets of homemade scones and muffins you made yourself or bought that morning from a good bakery. Platters of fresh fruit look beautiful and make people feel that they are starting the day with a "good for you" meal. Big platters of bagels and smoked salmon with cream cheese require no cooking at all and make the meal a special treat. A big bowl of homemade granola is wonderful alone with milk, or on top of fruit with yogurt. And the only thing left to do is set a gorgeous table and choose just the right Sunday-morning music.

The setting for breakfast can be a nice surprise. On a warm spring day, we take the kitchen table out to the garden among the tulips and have breakfast outdoors. On a beautiful summer morning, we put the coffee in thermoses, pack up the scones, and go sit on the beach to watch the sun come up. And in the winter, I set up a table with crisp white linens in front of a roaring fire in the study and serve hot oatmeal with great toppings. It feels so luxurious to me to start the day with close friends in a special setting, as if you don't have a care in the world.

the perfect cup of coffee

Everyone wants to know why the coffee at Barefoot Contessa is so good. I like to think it has something to do with the atmosphere in the store, but the truth is, the quality of the coffee beans is outstanding.

Buy the best-quality coffee beans you can afford and have the store grind them for your type of coffeemaker.

Measuring the coffee is the next important step. For each cup of water, as measured on the coffeemaker, use 1 level tablespoon of ground coffee. I use a quick-measuring method: figure out how much coffee you need in *cup* measures, rather than in *tablespoon* measures (8 tablespoons equal a ½-cup measure). Therefore, if you make 8 cups of coffee each time, you can simply use a level ½-cup measure of ground coffee each time you make a pot. Instead of all that measuring while I'm still half asleep, I keep a cup measure with the ground coffee, and it comes out perfectly every time.

For storing coffee, I find that if I leave ground coffee in the freezer, measure it directly into the coffeemaker, and immediately return it to the freezer; the quality of the coffee is the same from the beginning of the bag to the end. You can also keep it in an airtight container on the counter. The key is that a minimum amount of air is allowed to come in contact with the ground coffee.

There are lots of varieties of coffee; make a blend that you like for different times of the day. Start with something mild and flavorful, such as Guatemalan or Costa Rican. Then add beans with more body, like French roast. Experiment and you'll find a blend that will satisfy you for years.

homemade granola

This is the best granola. It was inspired by the delicious granola in Sarah Chase's Open House Cookbook. *I started with her recipe and then added dried apricots, dried figs, dried cherries, dried cranberries, and roasted cashews. I love it sprinkled over yogurt and berries, but in a bowl with cold milk, it's just fine, too.*

4 CUPS	old-fashioned rolled oats
2 CUPS	sweetened, shredded coconut
2 CUPS	sliced almonds
¾ CUP	vegetable oil
½ CUP	good honey
1½ CUPS	small-diced dried apricots
1 CUP	small-diced dried figs
1 CUP	dried cherries
1 CUP	dried cranberries
1 CUP	roasted, unsalted cashews

Preheat the oven to 350 degrees.

Toss the oats, coconut, and almonds together in a large bowl. Whisk together the oil and honey in a small bowl. Pour the liquids over the oat mixture and stir with a wooden spoon until all the oats and nuts are coated. Pour onto a 13 × 18-inch baking sheet. Bake, stirring occasionally with a spatula, until the mixture turns a nice, even golden brown, about 45 minutes.

Remove the granola from the oven and allow to cool, stirring occasionally. Add the apricots, figs, cherries, cranberries, and cashews. Store the cooled granola in an airtight container.

banana crunch muffins

MAKES 18 LARGE MUFFINS

This muffin is the perfect balance of moist muffin and crunchy surprises.
It is important to use really ripe bananas to get the best flavor.

3 CUPS	*all-purpose flour*
2 CUPS	*sugar*
2 TEASPOONS	*baking powder*
1 TEASPOON	*baking soda*
½ TEASPOON	*salt*
½ POUND	*unsalted butter, melted and cooled*
2	*extra-large eggs*
¾ CUP	*whole milk*
2 TEASPOONS	*pure vanilla extract*
1 CUP	*mashed ripe bananas (2 bananas)*
1 CUP	*medium-diced ripe bananas (1 banana)*
1 CUP	*small-diced walnuts*
1 CUP	*granola*
1 CUP	*sweetened shredded coconut*
	Dried banana chips, granola, or shredded coconut (optional)

Preheat the oven to 350 degrees.

Line 18 large muffin cups with paper liners. Sift the flour, sugar, baking powder, baking soda, and salt into the bowl of an electric mixer fitted with a paddle attachment. Add the melted butter and blend. Combine the eggs, milk, vanilla, and mashed bananas, and add them to the flour-and-butter mixture. Scrape the bowl and blend well. Don't overmix.

Fold the diced bananas, walnuts, granola, and coconut into the batter. Spoon the batter into the paper liners, filling each one to the top. Top each muffin with dried banana chips, granola, or coconut, if desired. Bake for 25 to 30 minutes, or until the tops are brown and a toothpick comes out clean. Cool slightly, remove from the pan, and serve.

raspberry corn muffins

MAKES 12 LARGE MUFFINS

We all know how dry most corn muffins can be, which is why this moist and flavorful muffin is so popular. We pipe good raspberry preserves into the middle.

3 CUPS	*all-purpose flour*
1 CUP	*sugar*
1 CUP	*medium cornmeal*
2 TABLESPOONS	*baking powder*
1½ TEASPOONS	*salt*
1½ CUPS	*whole milk*
½ POUND	*unsalted butter, melted and cooled*
2	*extra-large eggs*
¾ CUP	*good raspberry preserves*

These muffins are also delicious without the raspberry preserves.

Preheat the oven to 350 degrees.

Line 12 large muffin cups with paper liners. In the bowl of an electric mixer fitted with a paddle attachment, mix the flour, sugar, cornmeal, baking powder, and salt. In a separate bowl, combine the milk, melted butter, and eggs. With the mixer on the lowest speed, pour the wet ingredients into the dry ones and stir until they are *just* blended. Spoon the batter into the paper liners, filling each one to the top. Bake for 30 minutes, until the tops are crisp and a toothpick comes out clean. Cool slightly and remove from the pan.

After the muffins cool, spoon the raspberry preserves into a pastry bag fitted with a large round tip. Push thc tip of the bag through the top of the muffin and squeeze 1 to 2 tablespoons of preserves into the middle. Repeat for each muffin.

cranberry harvest muffins

MAKES 18 LARGE MUFFINS

This wonderful autumn recipe comes from Sarah Chase's Open House Cookbook, *which has inspired me for years. She had a famous store appropriately called Que Sera Sarah, on Nantucket, where cranberries are harvested. We have made these muffins thousands of times at Barefoot Contessa and they are a hit every time.*

3 CUPS	*all-purpose flour*
1 TABLESPOON	*baking powder*
½ TEASPOON	*baking soda*
½ TEASPOON	*salt*
1 TABLESPOON	*ground cinnamon*
2 TEASPOONS	*ground ginger*
1¼ CUPS	*whole milk*
2	*extra-large eggs*
½ POUND	*unsalted butter, melted and cooled*
1½ CUPS	*coarsely chopped fresh cranberries*
½ CUP	*medium-diced Calimyrna figs*
¾ CUP	*coarsely chopped hazelnuts, toasted and skinned*
¾ CUP	*brown sugar, packed*
¾ CUP	*granulated sugar*

Preheat the oven to 375 degrees.

Line 18 muffin cups with paper liners. Sift together the flour, baking powder, baking soda, salt, cinnamon, and ginger in a large bowl. Make a well in the center of the mixture and add the milk, eggs, and melted butter. Stir quickly just to combine. Add the cranberries, figs, hazelnuts, and both sugars and stir just to distribute the fruits, nuts, and sugar evenly throughout the batter.

Spoon the batter into the paper liners, filling each one to the top. Bake for 20 to 25 minutes, until browned on the top and a toothpick comes out clean.

Greasing the top of the muffin pan will make it easier to take the muffins out.

This batter can be made a day ahead, and scooped and baked before breakfast.

cheddar-dill scones

MAKES 16 LARGE SCONES

Years ago, a food writer from the New York Times *called to ask if we made our famous scones in different flavors. I said, "Oh, yes, we make cheddar-dill scones and strawberry scones." Of course, I had never made either one, so I immediately went to work to create both recipes. They have been on the menu at Barefoot Contessa ever since.*

4 CUPS	*plus 1 tablespoon all-purpose flour*
2 TABLESPOONS	*baking powder*
2 TEASPOONS	*salt*
¾ POUND	*cold unsalted butter, diced*
4	*extra-large eggs, beaten lightly*
1 CUP	*cold heavy cream*
½ POUND	*extra-sharp yellow cheddar cheese, small-diced*
1 CUP	*minced fresh dill*
1	*egg beaten with 1 tablespoon water or milk, for egg wash*

White cheddar is usually sharper, but yellow cheddar looks better in the scones.

Be sure the dill is free of all sand before you add it.

Preheat the oven to 400 degrees.

Combine 4 cups of flour, the baking powder, and salt in the bowl of an electric mixer fitted with a paddle attachment. Add the butter and mix on low speed until the butter is in pea-sized pieces. Mix the eggs and heavy cream and quickly add them to the flour-and-butter mixture. Combine until *just* blended. Toss together the cheddar, dill, and 1 tablespoon of flour and add them to the dough. Mix until they are almost incorporated.

Dump the dough onto a well-floured surface and knead it for 1 minute, until the cheddar and dill are well distributed. Roll the dough ¾-inch thick. Cut into 4-inch squares and then in half diagonally to make triangles. Brush the tops with egg wash. Bake on a baking sheet lined with parchment paper for 20 to 25 minutes, until the outside is crusty and the inside is fully baked.

strawberry scones

MAKES 14 TO 16 LARGE SCONES

*I made scones for a week before I came up with a recipe that would get
customers out of their beds in the morning and into the store. This is it.
In a world where most scones are like hockey pucks, this is light and moist.
We use all kinds of fruit fillings, including raisins, fresh cranberries, and
dried cherries. The key to flaky scones is to not overblend the butter.*

4 CUPS	*plus 1 tablespoon all-purpose flour*
2 TABLESPOONS	*sugar, plus additional for sprinkling*
2 TABLESPOONS	*baking powder*
2 TEASPOONS	*salt*
¾ POUND	*cold unsalted butter, diced*
4	*extra-large eggs, lightly beaten*
1 CUP	*cold heavy cream*
¾ CUP	*small-diced dried strawberries*
1	*egg beaten with 2 tablespoons water or milk, for egg wash*

*Dried strawberries
are available in
specialty food stores
or by mail order.*

Preheat the oven to 400 degrees.

In the bowl of an electric mixer fitted with a paddle attachment,
combine 4 cups of flour, 2 tablespoons sugar, baking powder, and
salt. Blend in the cold butter at the lowest speed and mix until the
butter is in pea-sized pieces. Combine the eggs and heavy cream
and quickly add them to the flour-and-butter mixture. Combine
until *just* blended. Toss the strawberries with 1 tablespoon of
flour, add them to the dough, and mix quickly. The dough may
be a bit sticky.

Dump the dough out onto a well-floured surface and be sure

it is well combined. Flour your hands and a rolling pin and roll the dough ¾-inch thick. You should see lumps of butter in the dough. Cut into squares with a 4-inch plain or fluted cutter, and then cut them in half diagonally to make triangles. Place on a baking sheet lined with parchment paper.

Brush the tops with egg wash. Sprinkle with sugar and bake for 20 to 25 minutes, until the outsides are crisp and the insides are fully baked.

maple-oatmeal scones

MAKES 14 LARGE SCONES

This is another variation of our famous scones, but with the addition of whole-wheat flour and oatmeal (to give it texture), pure maple syrup (to give it sweetness), and buttermilk (to make it lower in fat). Who wouldn't want to wake up to these in the morning?

3½ CUPS	*all-purpose flour*
1 CUP	*whole-wheat flour*
1 CUP	*quick-cooking oats, plus additional for sprinkling*
2 TABLESPOONS	*baking powder*
2 TABLESPOONS	*granulated sugar*
2 TEASPOONS	*salt*
1 POUND	*cold unsalted butter, diced*
½ CUP	*cold buttermilk*
½ CUP	*pure maple syrup*
4	*extra-large eggs, lightly beaten*
1	*egg beaten with 1 tablespoon milk or water, for egg wash*

GLAZE

1¼ CUPS	*confectioners' sugar*
½ CUP	*pure maple syrup*
1 TEASPOON	*pure vanilla extract*

I like McCann's quick-cooking Irish oatmeal for this recipe, but Quaker's is fine, too.

There is no substitute for the flavor of pure maple syrup.

continued next page

Preheat the oven to 400 degrees.

In the bowl of an electric mixer fitted with a paddle attachment, combine the flours, oats, baking powder, sugar, and salt. Blend the cold butter in at the lowest speed and mix until the butter is in pea-sized pieces. Combine the buttermilk, maple syrup, and eggs and add quickly to the flour-and-butter mixture. Mix until *just* blended. The dough may be sticky.

Dump the dough out onto a well-floured surface and be sure it is combined. Flour your hands and a rolling pin and roll the dough ³/₄- to 1-inch thick. You should see lumps of butter in the dough. Cut into 3-inch rounds with a plain or fluted cutter and place on a baking sheet lined with parchment paper.

Brush the tops with egg wash. Bake for 20 to 25 minutes, until the tops are crisp and the insides are done.

To make the glaze, combine the confectioners' sugar, maple syrup, and vanilla. When the scones are done, cool for 5 minutes, and drizzle each scone with 1 tablespoon of glaze. I like to sprinkle some uncooked oats on the top, for garnish. The warmer the scones are when you glaze them, the thinner the glaze will be.

Add ³/₄ cup of raisins or small-diced pecans to give this scone a different flavor.

Scones can be cut out ahead of time, stored in the refrigerator for a few days, and baked just before serving.

hot chocolate

MAKES 5 CUPS; SERVES 4 TO 5

Who doesn't love *hot chocolate on a cold winter day? This hot chocolate has wonderful depth of flavor from two kinds of chocolate, pure vanilla, and espresso. I sometimes even serve it for dessert with whipped cream, but it's good anytime, especially for Sunday breakfast. Ummm.*

2½ CUPS	*whole milk*
2 CUPS	*half-and-half*
4 OUNCES	*bittersweet chocolate, chopped*
4 OUNCES	*milk chocolate, chopped*
1 TABLESPOON	*sugar*
1 TEASPOON	*pure vanilla extract*
1 TEASPOON	*instant espresso or coffee powder*
4 TO 5	*vanilla beans or cinnamon sticks*

Heat the milk and half-and-half in a saucepan on medium heat to just below the simmering point. Remove the pan from the heat and add both chocolates. When the chocolates are melted, add the sugar, vanilla extract, and espresso and whisk vigorously. Reheat gently and serve immediately. Use a vanilla bean or cinnamon stick to garnish each serving.

The better the chocolate, the better the drink. Fine bakers use Valrhôna from France or Callebaut from Belgium, but Hershey's will work, too.

white hot chocolate

MAKES 9 CUPS; SERVES 8 TO 10

If traditional hot chocolate is so delicious and comforting, I thought, why not white hot chocolate? Nothing could be easier, and it is very satisfying on a cold winter day.

4 CUPS	*whole milk*
4 CUPS	*half-and-half*
1 POUND	*white chocolate, chopped*
2 TEASPOONS	*pure vanilla extract*
8 TO 10	*vanilla beans*

I love to serve hot chocolate in those big café au lait bowls they use at French bistros. They are available from Williams-Sonoma (page 244).

In a saucepan on medium heat, heat the milk and half-and-half to just below the simmering point. Remove the pan from the heat and add the white chocolate. When the chocolate is melted, add the vanilla and whisk vigorously. Reheat very gently and serve with a vanilla bean as a stirrer in each cup.

White chocolate is the "vanilla" alternative to traditional hot chocolate.

orange yogurt

With just a little bit of planning, this yogurt takes only a few minutes to make. Some of the liquid is drained out of the plain yogurt and replaced with fresh orange juice to add more flavor. I love the chunkiness of all the additions. Use this recipe as a base and make up new flavors, such as cranberry orange or maple walnut.

1 QUART	*plain low-fat yogurt*
¼ CUP	*raisins*
¼ CUP	*chopped walnuts*
1½ TEASPOONS	*pure vanilla extract*
¼ CUP	*good honey*
	Grated zest of 1 orange
½ TO 1 CUP	*freshly squeezed orange juice*
	Orange, orange zest, raisins, or walnuts (optional)

I prefer low-fat to nonfat yogurt for this recipe.

Line a sieve with cheesecloth or paper towels and suspend it over a bowl. Pour the yogurt into the sieve and allow it to drain, refrigerated, for 3 hours or overnight.

Place the thickened yogurt into a medium bowl and add the raisins, walnuts, vanilla, honey, and orange zest to taste. Thin with orange juice until it is a desirable consistency. Garnish with sections of orange, extra orange zest, raisins, or walnuts and serve.

fresh fruit platter

The most important thing about making one of these platters is choosing ripe, seasonal fruit. After that, it's just cutting and arranging. For 10 to 12 people, this is a suggested list of ingredients:

2 *small ripe melons*

1 *"golden" pineapple*

2 *bunches grapes*

1 PINT *fresh figs*

1 PINT *raspberries*

1 PINT *strawberries*

1 PINT *blueberries*

1 *red papaya*

I like to begin the platter with a base of ripe, colorful, sliced melons and pineapple—for example, cantaloupe, honeydew, Galia, or Cavaillon melons, plus the new "golden" pineapples. Peel the outside of a whole melon, cut it in half through the stem end, and scoop out the seeds. Place the melon halves cut side down on a board, and slice them straight across into ½-inch-thick slices. Fan each half-melon out slightly and arrange it on the platter. Next, cut off the top and bottom of the pineapple, peel the outside, and use a sharp knife to remove the "eyes." Cut the pineapple in half lengthwise and remove the core by cutting a "V" down the center of each half. Again, place the pineapple halves, cut side down, on a board and slice them straight across into ½-inch-thick slices. Fan the slices out and arrange them next to the melon on the platter.

Once the base is set, you can add any kind of fruit that's available. I like to have one thing that is taller than the rest, such as a large bunch of grapes or a decoratively cut papaya, to give the platter height. Then I add raspberries, strawberries, blueberries, and fresh figs in casual but organized groups. The platter can look like a bowl of M&M's if there are too many colors scattered with no order. Visually, your eye needs to have a focal point and to be able to see each type of fruit. After all the fruit is arranged, I add flat green leaves around the outside of the fruit, to set off the colors. Use lemon and galax leaves from your florist, or fig leaves and grape leaves from your garden. Make sure they are pesticide-free and well washed.

Any kind of fruit will work well on this platter. For special occasions, add persimmons, kiwi, passion fruit, Queen Anne cherries, fresh apricots, and mangos. Choose whatever is colorful and seasonal. What a healthy way to start the day!

assembling party food

Despite all the time I have spent cooking at Barefoot Contessa, at home I think of myself as someone who assembles rather than cooks. I love to shop for delicious ingredients and serve them "as is."

Years ago a catering client asked us to end a very elegant dinner with ice cream sundaes—complete with hot chocolate sauce, fresh raspberries, M&M's, and crumbled Oreos. I knew right away that this idea was brilliant. All the guests loosened up and had a terrific time making their own desserts. And the caterer didn't even have to cook!

In this list, I have grouped ingredients you can assemble at home to make wonderful courses that are both simple and delicious.

APPETIZERS

Potato chips

Pistachios

Oil-cured olives

Caviar

Cavaillon melon

Prosciutto

Italian bread

Norwegian
  smoked salmon

Brown bread

Honey mustard or
  herbed butter

Farmhouse
  cheddar cheese

Mango chutney

Crackers

Apples

Smoked chicken

Horseradish sauce

Cherry tomatoes

Parmesan cheese

Pears

Bread sticks

Smoked mozzarella

Cracked pepper
  and olive oil

Semolina bread

Endive leaves

Gorgonzola

Toasted walnuts

Caviar

Blinis

Crème fraîche

Stuffed grape
  leaves

Feta cheese

Toasted pita bread

Smoked trout

Horseradish sauce

SALADS

Shaved fennel

Grated carrots

Grated radicchio

Lemon vinaigrette

Endive leaves

Blue cheese

Walnuts

Walnut vinaigrette

Arugula

Lemon vinaigrette

Shaved Parmesan

Tomatoes

Mozzarella

Olive oil

Pesto

Diced endive leaves

Diced avocado

Creamy vinaigrette

DESSERTS

Pound cake
Lemon curd
Strawberries

Fresh berries
Honey vanilla
   crème fraîche
Cookies

Vanilla ice cream
Diced candied
   ginger
Ginger snaps

Chocolate sorbet
Biscotti
Vin Santo

Fresh lychees on ice

Vanilla ice cream
Blood-orange
   sorbet

Apples
Cheddar cheese
Oatmeal cookies

½ cantaloupe
   filled with
   Sauternes

Gorgonzola
Lavender honey
Toasted walnuts

Pears
Parmesan cheese

Ice cream soda:
   coffee ice cream
   chocolate sauce
   club soda

Ice cream soda:
   Vanilla ice cream
   Vanilla liqueur
   Club soda

White peaches
Macaroons

Pears
Ginger cookies

Stilton
Crackers
Aged Port

Long-stemmed
   strawberries
Sour cream
Brown sugar

Ice cream
   sandwiches:
   ginger snaps with
   vanilla ice cream

Pound cake
Strawberries
Orange segments
Chocolate ganache

Blood oranges
Amaretti

Meringue shells
Raspberries
Whipped cream

sources for serving
platters, tableware, and
kitchen equipment

As you'll have seen, I think platters are just about indispensable. I'm a New York girl, and I can't pretend the list that follows is comprehensive. If you're near these locations, by all means visit them. You are sure to have favorite shops in your area, and you can talk to the owner about finding special things for you. And don't overlook flea markets and tag sales.

As for decorating those platters, lemon leaves and galax leaves are ideal finishing touches and a staple of all good florists.

NEW YORK CITY

Barneys New York
660 Madison Avenue
New York, NY 10021
212-826-8900
*Fine silver and
contemporary china
and pottery.*

Bardith
901 Madison Avenue
New York, NY 10021
212-737-3775
*Antique china and
pottery platters, mostly
English, before 1860.
Exceptional.*

Bergdorf Goodman
754 Fifth Avenue
New York, NY 10019
212-753-7300
*The most extensive
collection of beautiful
platters, including fine
silver, hotel silver, fine
china, Asian pottery,
and modern design.*

Bridge Kitchenware
214 East 52nd Street
New York, NY 10022
212-688-4220
*A few restaurant platters,
but the most complete line
of cookware in the country,
including cast-iron "stove-
top" grills, doilies, marble
rounds and wood boards for
cheese platters, large muffin
tins, feuillette cutters for
scones, square and round
tart pans, French bread
baskets. They will ship.*

Christofle
680 Madison Avenue
New York, NY 10021
212-308-9390
*The finest silver and china
platters. Expensive.*

David Stypmann
190 Sixth Avenue
(near Prince)
New York, NY 10013
212-226-5717
Antique platters.

Dean & Deluca
560 Broadway
New York, NY 10012
212-226-6800
*Simple, contemporary
platters, plus doilies and
muffin cups.*

Fishs Eddy
889 Broadway
New York, NY 10003
212-420-9020
*"Restaurant" china
platters.*

The Mediterranean Shop
780 Madison Avenue
New York, NY 10021
212-879-3120
*French and Italian hand-
painted pottery platters.*

Tiffany & Co.
727 Fifth Avenue
New York, NY 10022
212-755-8000
*Silver, glass, and fine
English china platters.*

Tuscan Square
Rockefeller Center
16 West 51st Street
New York, NY 10020
212-977-7777
*Beautiful pottery platters in
Tuscan colors and pat-
terns. They have chargers,
which are very flat platters
used as "lay" plates, but are
also excellent for cheese,
salad, and dessert platters.
Highly recommended.*

Vito Giallo
222 East 83rd Street
New York, NY 10028
212-535-9885
*Most unusual collection
of antique platters and
tableware. By appointment.*

William Wayne Co.
846 Lexington Avenue
New York, NY 10021
212-737-8934
and
40 University Place
New York, NY 10003
212-533-4711
*Contemporary selection of
platters and baskets.*

Wolfman-Gold & Good
Company
117 Mercer Street
New York, NY 10012
212-431-1888
*Extraordinary collection of
platters, plus doilies and
paper leaves for decorating.*

Zona
97 Greene Street
New York, NY 10012
212-925-6750
*Contemporary pottery
and platters with a
Southwestern flair.*

NEW YORK STATE
Curly Willow
55 Main Street
East Hampton, NY 11937
516-324-1122
*Contemporary platters in
extraordinary colors.*

English Country Antiques
Snake Hollow Road
Bridgehampton, NY
11932
516-537-0606
and
21 Newtown Lane
East Hampton, NY 11937
516-329-5773
*Antique ironstone and
English transferware.*

Fishs Eddy
41 Job's Lane
Southampton, NY 11968
516-287-2993
"Restaurant" china platters.

Hunters and Collectors
Poxabogue Lane
Bridgehampton, NY
11932
516-537-4233
Antique platters.

The Monogram Shop
11 Newtown Lane
East Hampton, NY 11937
516-329-3397
*Beautiful antiques and
monogrammed tableware.*

Sage Street Antiques
Sage Street
Sag Harbor, NY 11963
516-725-4036
*Continually changing
collection of antique
glass, ironstone, and
transferware platters.*

Zona
Newtown Lane
East Hampton, NY 11937
516-324-4100
*Contemporary pottery
platters.*

SAN FRANCISCO AREA
Draeger's
1010 University Drive
Menlo Park, CA 94025
650-688-0688
*Full housewares department
that also carries serving
platters.*

Gump's
135 Post Street
San Francisco, CA 94108
415-982-1616
800-766-7628
*Silver, china, and
crystal serving platters
in all price ranges.*

LOS ANGELES AREA

Cottura
10250 Santa Monica Blvd.
#112
Los Angeles, CA 90067
310-277-3828
*Rustic Italian platters
and tableware.*

Dishes a la Carte
5650 West Third Street
(La Brea)
Los Angeles, CA 90036
213-938-6223
*New pottery and
hand-painted platters.*

For the Table
357½ S. Robertson Blvd.
(Charleville)
Beverly Hills, CA 90210
310-659-3111
*Vintage and new platters,
specializing in unusual
items, such as Paolo
Buffetti from Italy.*

Geary's
351 N. Beverly Drive
(Brighton)
Beverly Hills, CA 90210
310-273-4741
*Extensive selection of fine
china and silver platters
since 1930.*

Hollyhock
214 N. Larchmont Blvd.
Los Angeles, CA 90004
213-931-3400
*Unusual selection of
new and antique platters
and tableware.*

Jordano's
3025 DeLaVina Street
Santa Barbara, CA 93105
805-569-6262
*Pottery and china platters
and tableware.*

Maison et Cafe
148 South La Brea
Los Angeles, CA 90036
213-935-3157
French platters.

Room with a View
1600 Montana Avenue
(16th)
Santa Monica, CA 90403
310-998-5858
*Lovely Cucina Fresca
Italian pottery, hotel silver,
and other china platters.*

NATIONAL STORES

Crate & Barrel
800-323-5461
*Large selection of
reasonably priced,
beautiful platters.*

Royal China and
Porcelain Company
800-631-7120, for a store
near you
*Transferware porcelain
platters and serving pieces.*

Sur La Table
84 Pine Street
Seattle, WA 98101
800-243-0852
*Line of kitchenware,
including some platters
and chargers. Catalog,
plus retail stores.*

Williams-Sonoma
800-541-2233
*Nice selection of white
and patterned ceramic
platters, plus doilies and
paper muffin-cup liners.*

sources for
mail-order
specialty foods

A.L. Bazzini
200 Food Center Drive
Bronx, NY 10474
718-842-8644
800-228-0172
Dried fruits and nuts, fruit and nut mixtures, plus nut brittles and candies.

Alleva Dairy
188 Grand Street
New York, NY 10013
212-226-7990
800-425-5382
Outstanding freshly made mozzarella, smoked mozzarella, and mozzarella di bufala.

American Spoon Food
P.O. Box 566
Petoskey, MI 49770
800-222-5886
Fruit preserves and butters, barbecue sauces, chutneys, dried cherries, dried cran-berries, pepper jelly, pancake mixes, and maple syrup.

Balducci's
424 Avenue of the Americas
New York, NY 10011
212-673-2600
800-255-3822
Full line of specialty foods and ingredients, including fresh sausage, filet of beef, smoked salmon, prepared foods, and desserts.

Barefoot Contessa
46 Newtown Lane
East Hampton, NY 11937
516-324-0240
Full line of specialty foods and coffees.

Cafe Fanny
1619 Fifth Street
Berkeley, CA 94710
800-441-5413 ext. 1
Alice Waters's famous granola.

D'Artagnan
399 St. Paul Avenue
Jersey City, NJ 07306
201-792-0748
800-DARTAGNAN
Fresh foie gras, free-range poultry, specialty meats, prepared terrines, and pâtés and demi-glace.

Dean & Deluca
560 Broadway
New York, NY 10012
212-226-6800
and
3276 M Street NW
Washington, DC 20007
202-342-2500
and
6903 Phillips Place Court
Charlotte, NC
704-643-6868
and
607 South Street
Helena Highway
St. Helena, CA
707-967-9980

www.dean-deluca.com
catalog orders:
800-221-7714
Outstanding line of specialty foods, specialty ingredients, and cookware.

Divine Delights
24 Digital Drive, Suite 10
Novato, CA 94949
800-443-2836
Handmade petits fours and truffles, plus seasonal specialties.

Down East Seafood
Express
Box 138
Brookville, ME 04617
800-556-2326
Maine lobsters, sea scallops, and crabmeat delivered overnight.

Ducktrap River Fish
Farm
RFD#2 Box 378
Lincolnville, ME 04849
207-763-3960
Smoked eastern and western salmon.

E.A.T.
1064 Madison Avenue
New York, NY 10028
212-772-0022
Eli Zabar's outstanding specialty foods, including smoked salmon, caviar, gift baskets, and pastry. They've even shipped chicken soup to California!

Eli's Bread
1064 Madison Avenue
New York, NY 10028
212-772-2011
*Eli Zabar's outstanding
and extensive line of freshly
baked breads, including
health bread and raisin nut
bread for tea sandwiches.*

Eli's Manhattan
1411 Third Avenue
New York, NY 10028
212-717-8100
*Eli Zabar's newest specialty
store, including meats, fish,
and produce.*

Ideal Cheese Shop
1205 Second Avenue
New York, NY 10021
212-688-7579
800-382-0109
*Large selection of domestic
and international cheeses,
plus olives from Provence,
Scottish smoked salmon,
and specialty cured meats.*

King Arthur Flour
The Baker's Catalogue
Norwich, VT
800-827-6836
*Terrific source for excellent
flours, specialty grains, dried
fruit and nuts, and baking
ingredients, plus a large line
of professional bakeware.*

Les Trois Petits Cochons
453 Greenwich Street
New York, NY 10013
212-219-1230
800-537-7283
*Fresh pâtés, terrines, ham,
and cornichons.*

Martha by Mail
Martha Stewart Living
800-950-7130
*An ever-expanding
catalog of foods, cooking
supplies, and "good things"
for entertaining.*

New York Cake and
Baking Distributors
56 West 22nd Street
New York, NY 10010
212-675-2253
800-942-2539
*Full line of baking and
decorating supplies.*

Out of a Flower
703 McKinney #202
Dallas, TX 75202
800-743-4696
*Outstanding homemade
fruit and herb sorbets and
ice creams, plus seasonal
specialties.*

Petrossian
419 West 13th Street
New York, NY 10014
800-828-9241
*Fine caviar, foie gras, smoked
salmon, smoked sturgeon,
blinis, and other delicacies.*

Sarabeth's Kitchen
2291 Second Avenue
New York, NY 10035
800-773-7378
*Extraordinary homemade
preserves, baked goods,
and granola.*

Shelburne Farms
102 Harbor Road
Shelburne, VT 05482
802-985-8686
*Farmhouse cheddar
cheeses, mustards, and
spiral-cut hams.*

Vermont Butter and
Cheese
Pittman Road
Websterville, VT 05678
800-884-6287
*Fresh goat cheeses plus
crème fraîche, fromage
blanc, and cheese tortas.*

Virginia Diner
Wakefield, VA 23888
800-868-6887
*Specialty peanuts, peanut
brittle, pecans, and desserts.*

Williams-Sonoma
San Francisco, CA
800-541-2233
*Specialty ingredients,
including oils, vinegars,
pastas, sauces, and baking
supplies.*

index

Appetizers, 39–66
  Crab Cakes, 44
  Fruit and Cheese Platter, 64
  Grilled Lemon Chicken, 48
  Guacamole, 50
  Hummus, 46
  Lamb Sausage in Puff
    Pastry, 42
  Lobster Salad in Endive, 43
  menu planning with, 39
  Pan-Fried Onion Dip, 53
  Roasted Eggplant Spread, 41
  simple suggestions for, 238
  Smoked Salmon Tea
    Sandwiches, 56
  Sun-Dried Tomato Dip, 54
  Turkey Tea Sandwiches, 58
  Vegetable Sushi, 61
Applesauce, Homemade, 155

Baked Virginia Ham, 119
Banana Crunch Muffins, 212
Barbecue Sauce, 121
Barbecued Chicken, 120
Basil Soup, Roasted-Tomato, 84
Beans, dried
  Hummus, 46
  Lentil Vegetable Soup, 80
  Split Pea Soup, Parker's, 73
  White Bean Soup,
    Rosemary, 83
Beans, Green.
    See Haricots Verts
Beef Bourguignon,
    Filet of, 123
Beets with Orange Vinaigrette,
    93
Bell Peppers
  Grilled Lemon Chicken
    Salad, 99
  Roasted Vegetable Torte, 160
  Szechuan Noodles, 108
Beverages
  Fresh Lemonade, 32
  Hot Chocolate, 225
  Perfect Cup of Coffee, 209
  White Hot Chocolate, 226
Bread Pudding, Croissant, 192
Breakfast recipes, 207–32
  Banana Crunch Muffins, 212
  Cheddar-Dill Scones, 218
  Cranberry Harvest
    Muffins, 216

Fresh Fruit Platter, 231
Homemade Granola, 210
Hot Chocolate, 225
Maple-Oatmeal Scones, 223
Orange Yogurt, 229
The Perfect Cup of
    Coffee, 209
Raspberry Corn Muffins, 215
Strawberry Scones, 220
White Hot Chocolate, 226
Broccoli with Garlic, 100
Brownies, Outrageous, 172
Brussels Sprouts, Roasted, 150
Butter, Herb, 56
Buttercream, Chocolate, 196
Butternut Squash,
    Caramelized, 151

Cake, Chocolate
    Buttercream, 194
Capellini, Lemon,
    with Caviar, 129
Caramelized Butternut
    Squash, 151
Carrots
  Roasted, 149
  Vegetable Coleslaw, 107
Caviar, Lemon Capellini
    with, 129
Cheddar Corn Chowder, 74
Cheddar-Dill Scones, 218
Cheese
  Cheddar Corn Chowder, 74
  Cheddar-Dill Scones, 218
  Cream Cheese Icing, 176
  Parmesan Croutons, 87
  Parmesan Smashed
    Potatoes, 158
  Platter, Fruit and, 64
  Potato-Fennel Gratin, 156
  Roasted Fennel with
    Parmesan, 154
  Roasted Vegetable Torte, 160
  Scallion Cream Cheese, 58
  Spinach Pie, 163
Chicken
  Barbecued, 120
  Grilled Lemon, 48
  Indonesian Ginger, 125
  Roast, Perfect, 130
  Salad, Grilled Lemon, 99
Chiffonade, illustrated, 35
Chocolate
  Buttercream, 196
  Buttercream Cake, 194
  Hot, 225

Hot, White, 226
Outrageous Brownies, 172
Chopped food, illustrated, 35
Chowder, Cheddar Corn, 74
Clambake, Kitchen, 126
Cocktail parties
  guidelines for, 39
  simple foods for, 238
Coconut Cupcakes, 175
Coffee, The Perfect Cup of, 209
Coleslaw, Vegetable, 107
Cookies
  "Linzer," 178
  Outrageous Brownies, 172
  Pecan Shortbread, 181
  Pecan Squares, 188
  Shortbread Hearts, 177
Corn
  Chowder, Cheddar, 74
  Muffins, Raspberry, 215
  Salad, Fresh, 101
Country Dessert Platter, 200
Couscous, Curried, 94
Crab Cakes, 44
Cranberry Harvest Muffins, 216
Cream, Pastry, 197
Cream Cheese, Scallion, 58
Cream Cheese Icing, 176
Crème Fraîche,
    Honey Vanilla, 198
Crisp, Peach and Raspberry, 190
Croissant Bread Pudding, 192
Croutons, Parmesan, 87
Crudité Platter, 111
Cupcakes, Coconut, 175
Curried Couscous, 94

Dessert Platter, Country, 200
Desserts, 171–203
  Chocolate Buttercream
    Cake, 194
  Coconut Cupcakes, 175
  Country Dessert Platter, 200
  Croissant Bread Pudding, 192
  Fresh Fruit Tart, 184
  Honey Vanilla Crème
    Fraîche, 198
  Lime Curd Tart, 187
  "Linzer" Cookies, 178
  Outrageous Brownies, 172
  Pastry Cream, 197
  Peach and Raspberry
    Crisp, 190
  Pecan Shortbread, 181

Pecan Squares, 188
Raspberry Tart, 182
Shortbread Hearts, 177
simple suggestions for, 239
Diced food, illustrated, 34, 35
Dill Scones, Cheddar-, 218
Dinner Entrées, 117–42
    Baked Virginia Ham, 119
    Barbecued Chicken, 120
    Filet of Beef Bourguignon,
        123
    Grilled Lemon Chicken, 48
    Grilled Tuna Niçoise
        Platter, 140
    Indonesian Ginger
        Chicken, 125
    Kitchen Clambake, 126
    Lemon Capellini
        with Caviar, 129
    Lobster Potpie, 132
    Perfect Roast Chicken, 130
    Salmon with Fennel, 134
    Swordfish with Tomatoes
        and Capers, 136
    Turkey Meat Loaf, 138
Dipping Sauce, Sushi, 63
Dips and Spreads
    Hummus, 46
    Onion, Pan-Fried, 53
    Roasted Eggplant, 41
    Satay, 49
    Sun-Dried Tomato, 54

Eggplant
    Roasted, Spread, 41
    Roasted Vegetable Torte, 160
Endive, Lobster Salad in, 43
Entrées. *See* Dinner Entrées
Extract, Vanilla, 199

Fennel
    Gratin, Potato-, 156
    Roasted, with Parmesan, 154
    Salmon with, 134
    Soup, Roasted-Potato, 77
Filet of Beef Bourguignon, 123
Fingerling Potatoes, 159
Fish
    Grilled Salmon Salad, 102
    Grilled Tuna Niçoise
        Platter, 140
    Provençal Potato Salad, 98
    Salmon with Fennel, 134
    Smoked Salmon Tea
        Sandwiches, 56

Swordfish with Tomatoes
    and Capers, 136
French Onion Soup, 76
French Potato Salad, 96
Fresh Corn Salad, 101
Fresh Fruit Platter, 231
Fresh Fruit Tart, 184
Fresh Lemonade, 32
Frosting, Chocolate
    Buttercream, 196
Fruit. *See also specific fruits*
    and Cheese Platter, 64
    Platter, Fresh, 231
    Tart, Fresh, 184

Garlic, Broccoli with, 100
Gazpacho, 79
Ginger Chicken,
    Indonesian, 125
Glossary of kitchen terms, 34
Granola, Homemade, 210
Gratin, Potato-Fennel, 156
Grilled
    Lemon Chicken, 48
    Lemon Chicken Salad, 99
    Salmon Salad, 102
    Tuna Niçoise Platter, 140
    Vegetables, 166
Guacamole, 50

Ham, Baked Virginia, 119
Haricots Verts
    Grilled Tuna Niçoise
        Platter, 140
    Provençal Potato Salad, 98
Herb Butter, 56
Homemade Applesauce, 155
Homemade Granola, 210
Honey Vanilla Crème
    Fraîche, 198
Hot Chocolate, 225
Hot Chocolate, White, 226

Icing, Cream Cheese, 176
Indonesian Ginger Chicken, 125

Julienne, illustrated, 34

Kitchen Clambake, 126
Kitchen terms, glossary of, 34

Lamb Sausage in Puff Pastry, 42
Lemonade, Fresh, 32
Lemon(s)
    Capellini with Caviar, 129
    Chicken, Grilled, 48
    Chicken Salad, Grilled, 99
    Fresh Lemonade, 32

Lentil Vegetable Soup, 80
Lime Curd Tart, 187
"Linzer" Cookies, 178
Lobster
    Kitchen Clambake, 126
    Potpie, 132
    Salad in Endive, 43

Maple-Oatmeal Scones, 223
Meat Loaf, Turkey, 138
Minced food, illustrated, 35
Muffins
    Banana Crunch, 212
    Cranberry Harvest, 216
    Rašpberry Corn, 215

Noodles, Szechuan, 108

Oatmeal Scones, Maple-, 223
Onion
    Dip, Pan-Fried, 53
    Soup, French, 76
Orange
    Vinaigrette, Beets with, 93
    Yogurt, 229
Outrageous Brownies, 172

Pan-Fried Onion Dip, 53
Parker's Split Pea Soup, 73
Parmesan
    Croutons, 87
    Roasted Fennel with, 154
    Roasted Vegetable Torte, 160
    Smashed Potatoes, 158
Party foods, simple suggestions
    for, 238–39
Pasta
    Lemon Capellini
        with Caviar, 129
    Szechuan Noodles, 108
Pastry Cream, 197
Peach and Raspberry Crisp, 190
Peas, Sugar Snap. *See* Sugar
    Snap Peas
Pecan Shortbread, 181
Pecan Squares, 188
Peppers. *See* Bell Peppers
Perfect Cup of Coffee, 209
Perfect Roast Chicken, 130
Pie. *See also* Tart
    Lobster Potpie, 132
    Spinach, 163
Platters
    Country Dessert, 200
    Crudité, 111
    Fresh Fruit, 231

Fruit and Cheese, 64
Grilled Tuna Niçoise, 140
Vegetable, 164
Potato(es)
Cheddar Corn Chowder, 74
-Fennel Gratin, 156
Fingerling, 159
Grilled Tuna Niçoise
Platter, 140
Kitchen Clambake, 126
Parmesan Smashed, 158
Roasted-, Fennel Soup, 77
Salad, French, 96
Salad, Provençal, 98
Potpie, Lobster, 132
Provençal Potato Salad, 98
Pudding, Croissant Bread, 192
Puff Pastry, Lamb Sausage in,
42
Pumpkins, Baby, Roasted, 153

Raspberry
Corn Muffins, 215
Crisp, Peach and, 190
Tart, 182
Rémoulade Sauce, 45
Roast Chicken, Perfect, 130
Roasted
Baby Pumpkins, 153
Brussels Sprouts, 150
Carrots, 149
Eggplant Spread, 41
Fennel with Parmesan, 154
-Potato Fennel Soup, 77
-Tomato Basil Soup, 84
Vegetable Torte, 160
Vegetables, 166
Rosemary White Bean Soup, 83

Salad, 91–113
Beets with Orange
Vinaigrette, 93
Broccoli with Garlic, 100
Crudité Platter, 111
Curried Couscous, 94
French Potato, 96
Fresh Corn, 101
Grilled Lemon Chicken, 99
Grilled Salmon, 102
Lobster, in Endive, 43
Provençal Potato, 98
simple suggestions for, 238
Sugar Snap Peas with
Sesame, 105

Szechuan Noodles, 108
Vegetable Coleslaw, 107
Salmon
with Fennel, 134
Salad, Grilled, 102
Smoked, Tea Sandwiches, 56
Sandwiches, Tea
Smoked Salmon, 56
Turkey, 58
Satay Dip, 49
Sauce
Barbecue, 121
Dipping, Sushi, 63
Honey Vanilla Crème
Fraîche, 198
Rémoulade, 45
Sausage, Lamb,
in Puff Pastry, 42
Scallion Cream Cheese, 58
Scones
Cheddar-Dill, 218
Maple-Oatmeal, 223
Strawberry, 220
Seafood. *See* Fish; Shellfish
Sesame, Sugar Snap Peas
with, 105
Shellfish
Crab Cakes, 44
Kitchen Clambake, 126
Lobster Potpie, 132
Lobster Salad in Endive, 43
Shortbread, Pecan, 181
Shortbread Hearts, 177
Smoked Salmon Tea
Sandwiches, 56
Soup, 71–87
Cheddar Corn Chowder, 74
French Onion, 76
Gazpacho, 79
Lentil Vegetable, 80
Roasted-Potato Fennel, 77
Roasted-Tomato Basil, 84
Rosemary White Bean, 83
Split Pea, Parker's, 73
Spinach Pie, 163
Split Pea Soup, Parker's, 73
Spreads. *See* Dips and Spreads
Squares, Pecan, 188
Squash
Baby Pumpkins, Roasted, 153
Butternut, Caramelized, 151
Roasted Vegetable Torte, 160
Strawberry Scones, 220
Sugar Snap Peas
Grilled Lemon Chicken
Salad, 99
with Sesame, 105

Sun-Dried Tomato Dip, 54
Sushi, Vegetable, 61
Sushi Dipping Sauce, 63
Swordfish with Tomatoes and
Capers, 136
Szechuan Noodles, 108

Tart
Fresh Fruit, 184
Lime Curd, 187
Raspberry, 182
Tomato(es)
and Capers, Swordfish
with, 136
Gazpacho, 79
Grilled Tuna Niçoise
Platter, 140
Provençal Potato Salad, 98
Roasted-, Basil Soup, 84
Sun-Dried, Dip, 54
Torte, Roasted Vegetable, 160
Tuna
Grilled, Niçoise Platter, 140
Provençal Potato Salad, 98
Turkey
Meat Loaf, 138
Tea Sandwiches, 58

Vanilla
Crème Fraîche, Honey, 198
Extract, 199
Vegetable Coleslaw, 107
Vegetable Platter, 164
Vegetable Soup, Lentil, 80
Vegetable Sushi, 61
Vegetable Torte, Roasted, 160
Vegetables. *See also*
specific vegetables
Crudité Platter, 111
Gazpacho, 79
Grilled, 166
Roasted, 166
Vinaigrette, 113

White Bean Soup, Rosemary, 83
White Hot Chocolate, 226

Yogurt, Orange, 229